Canada, The Greatest Economy In the World?

THE FACTS YOU ARE NOT BEING TOLD
ABOUT YOUR MONEY. AND HOW TO
PROTECT YOURSELF FROM THE COMING
CRISIS.

John Thore Stub Sneisen

Couronne Publishing
WINNPEG, MANITOBA

Couronne Publishing Inc.
3377 Pembina Highway,
Winnipeg, Manitoba Canada
R3V1A2
www.couronnepublishing.com
support@couronnepublishing.com

Editing by: John Thore stub Sneisen and team.
All Referencing and Footnotes Created by the Author
Book Cover by: Vanessa Mendozzi
Interior Layout by: Couronne Publishing

Canada, The Greatest Economy In The World?/ John Thore Stub Sneisen. —1st ed.
ISBN 978-1-988497-05-1

Contents

I want to dedicate this book to my grandmother Else who has passed away and to my beautiful wife Quinn who always supports my work. To my wonderful parents Lolo and Johnny, my siblings Anne and Lars. My extended Canadian family and all my great friends' worldwide for connecting the dots. I want to thank all my family for supporting me through everything that I have done in life. I want to thank Osamede at Couronne Publishing for encouraging me to start writing.

I want to thank Josh for the fantastic foreword and for all the great work we have done up until now, but also into the future with World Alternative Media.

I want to thank G. Edward Griffin for being a great inspiration for me to share this information with you. I want to thank Freedom Force International for giving me the opportunity to interview and connect with some of the world's greatest minds when it comes to freedom and liberty.

I want to dedicate this book to you and hope that it wake you up to reality for the first time and which will help you to act and change yourself, your family and friends world for the better.

I want to thank many of my mentors along the way Rob Kirby, Jim Rickards, Peter Schiff, Robert Kiyosaki, Janet Tavakoli, Harry Dent, Mike Maloney, Nomi Prins, David Stockman, Russel Gray, Ralph T. Foster and 100's of economists, experts and people that lived through experiences in the past that lived to tell me the story I have to tell you today.

I want to thank Freedom Force International for giving me many mentors and experts to lean on and ask hard questions to. For many of them are the true beacons of light in the dark and hard to navigate financial world.

Foreword

Throughout the ages, servitude has been a heavily utilized religious practice of well-meaning people under the state's rule. The populace believes the new king is better than the old king and they enter a Hegelian circle, perpetuated by their own good intent as the grinning central planners, manipulators, and politicians flick their pens with dreams of further control.

First, monopolies are created through state favoring and subsidization. This is followed by people asking for new regulations and taxes to stifle the monopolies, thinking this will bring a more even ground to the marketplace. However, these new regulations and taxes create these monopolies, driving the small businesses out of the market, destroying true individual demand, muzzling competition and innovation. The good intent of those without knowledge simply creates a perpetual circle of servitude and blind belief.

So many individuals living in Canada feel free, safe and immune to the volatile dangers the world is plagued with. However, this is not the case. Canada, unbeknownst to most is not only susceptible to these dangers, but indeed one of the testing grounds for the globalist control complex quietly but vigorously hijacking both the markets and the monetary system.

John Sneisen, a member of Freedom Force International and World Alternative Media breaks down the effects of the Canadian monetary system and markets flawlessly with ease, leaving no stone unturned. John takes the complexity of the situation and makes it easy for people to understand, leaving people with an educated view of how the monetary system enslaves the populace.

Fear not! If you understand the problem and can call it by name, the solutions will be obvious. This isn't an end-time book. This is a guide for individuals to avoid the inevitable crash. This is a guide for individuals to ensure they can keep themselves and their families safe as the paper currency empire comes crashing down as it always has and always will. People too often miss what is right in front of them. The intrinsic nature of central planning and currency manipulation is always made up of temporary perks followed by long-term disaster. Imagine if you are falling down a bottomless pit of debt and being forced to ask the banking system or the government for a ladder up. This is the endgame of the global central banking cabal. Complete debt slavery. With knowledge, John gives you an alternative to this ultimatum. You don't have to depend on artificial markets and currency. You can stand as a free individual far above this storm and this book is an excellent start.

Josh Sigurdson,
Founder,
World Alternative Media Inc.

Is Canada The New Switzerland?

We have all heard how solid the banking system in Canada is! But are we being told the whole truth? Since I live in Canada, I thought I should take a deep look at how "Safe" Canada really is and how deeply embedded government and banking propaganda is, in Canadians Paradigms.

I recently read a great article that pokes holes in the propaganda Canadians are fed daily and I wanted to take a deep dive into this article and not just write about it, but give you a series of real proof of the dangers lurking in Canada. How Canada becomes this solid as they haven't in most cases gotten hit and hurt by the 2008 recession unless you had stocks which 90% of Canadians investing had.

Here are 12 points that I want to go through. They are very important as the truth about these points are not told to the public:

1. Bank Leverage
2. Bail In
3. Deposit Insurance
4. Central Bank Reserves
5. The Way Government in Canada Borrows Money
6. Banking and investment fees
7. Money Supply
8. Real Estate Construction as a Part of GDP
9. Debt
10. Commodities and Real Money
11. The CRA (Canada Revenue Agency) The Tax collectors
12. CPP (Canada Pension Plan)

Let's dive into the facts and numbers that will make you have a second thought about how solid the Canadian banks are and how much the government controls your life.

CHAPTER 1

Canadian Banks Secrecy and Leverage

First, bank leverage is calculated based on how much money have the banks created vs. how many deposits from customers do they have on their books. To clarify, as soon as you make a deposit into a savings or deposit account with your bank, you now borrow the money to your bank and the money is not yours anymore unless you choose to withdraw it from your bank and stuff that money into your mattress.

Here is an interesting piece of info that you might not know. Canada is one of the few countries where banks have zero capital requirements, meaning that when you deposit your money into the bank, the bank does not need to keep any money to keep your deposit safe and they can borrow 100% of your money to whomever they feel fit or invest it in whatever they want, either profitable or non-profitable investment or even leverage their already leveraged money.

(Figure 1.0)

Here is an excerpt from a working paper that the Bank of Canada has issued: Working Paper 97-8 / Document de travail 97-8: Implementation of Monetary Policy in a Regime with Zero Reserve Requirements: by Kevin Clinton

> Monetary policy can be implemented effectively with zero reserve requirements. Several countries now have no requirement, such as Australia, Belgium, Canada, Sweden and the United Kingdom. In others, including the United States and France, the level of minimum deposits at the central bank has fallen to very low levels, in large part because banks have found ways to avoid reserve requirements.This paper outlines a general framework for implementing mone-

tary policy in a regime with zero reserve requirements, focusing on the case of Canada.[1]

We looked at the bad leverage that Canadian Banks
can accrue, now how much have they racked up? Here is
a 2009 overview of how big of a leverage Canadian
banks have.

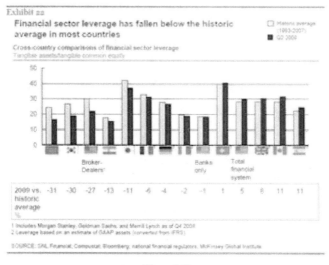

(Figure 1.1)

As you can see this was in 2008 and Canadian banks
didn't have leverage like most other banks did and today
some Canadian banks are leveraged as high as 50-60:1
meanwhile the average consumer has zero clue about
what is going on as Canadian banks continue to become
weaker and weaker through ZIRP and NIRP from Central Banks and cheap money leveraged into derivatives
which are set up to be further sold and leveraged and will

---

[1] Clinton, Kevin. Implementation of Monetary Policy in a Regime with Zero Reserve Requirements. Working paper. April 1997. Accessed January 4, 2016.
http://www.bankofcanada.ca/wp-content/uploads/2010/05/wp97-8.pdf.

fail, and what will happen thereafter? Bail INS or Bail Outs?

Canadian banks were believed not to be bailed out in the 2008 banking crash. I will show you evidence which proves that Canadian banking system was bailed out through the CMHC the Canadian TARP program, The US Federal Reserve and The Bank of Canada.

U.S. Federal Reserve Programs ($ Billions)		
	Average Daily Balance (Between 9/1/2008 and 4/8/2010)	Peak Day
Scotiabank	$3.6	$11.9
Royal Bank	$3.6	$8.8
TD Bank	$4.2	$8.4
CIBC	$0.8	$2.7
BMO	$0.5	$2.2

Source: Bloomberg

(Figure 1.2)[2]

Utilization of U.S. Fed Programs by Bank of Canada Eligible International Banks ($ Millions)							
	Term Auction Facility	Commercial Paper Funding Facility	Term Securities Lending Facility	Single Tranche Open Market Operations	Primary Dealer Credit	ABCP & Money Market Mutual Fund Liquidity Function	Discount Window
Bank of America Corp.	$15,632	$1,338	$2,122	$595	$936	$70	$20
BNP Paribas SA	$3,343	$301	$863	$2,663	$87	$0	$7
Deutsche Bank AG	$3,204	$0	$6,459	$2,818	$0	$0	$6
HSBC Holdings Plc	$152	$225	$80	$6	$0	$0	$0
ING Groep NV	$0	$978	$0	$0	$0	$0	$0
Merrill Lynch & Co. Inc.	$0	$722	$6,194	$341	$3,075	$0	$0
State Street Corp.	$2,205	$1,269	$0	$0	$0	$3,665	$1
Percentage of Total Program							
Bank of America Corp.	9%	2%	4%	3%	7%	1%	0%
BNP Paribas SA	2%	0%	2%	11%	1%	0%	0%
Deutsche Bank AG	2%	0%	12%	12%	0%	0%	0%
HSBC Holdings Plc	0%	0%	0%	0%	0%	0%	0%
ING Groep NV	0%	1%	0%	0%	0%	0%	0%
Merrill Lynch & Co. Inc.	0%	1%	8%	1%	24%	0%	0%
State Street Corp.	1%	2%	0%	0%	0%	35%	0%

Source: Bloomberg and author's calculations

(Figure 1.3)[3]

---

[2] Bloomberg Research

Through the Federal Reserve, Canadian bank received $33B as borrowed money from the FED. This was in December 2008. Here is a list showing the Canadian banks utilizing the FED for bailout of bad assets. (Figure 1.2)

Canadian	LVTS	Primary Dealer	Country
Bank of Montreal	x	x	Canada
Scotiabank	x	x	Canada
Canadian Imperial Bank of Commerce	x	x	Canada
Royal Bank of Canada	x	x	Canada
The Toronto-Dominion Bank	x	x	Canada
Alberta Treasury Branches	x		Canada
La Caisse centrale Desjardins du Québec	x	x	Canada
Central 1 Credit Union	x		Canada
Laurentian Bank of Canada	x	x	Canada
National Bank of Canada	x	x	Canada
Casgrain & Company Limited		x	Canada
Non-Canadian			
Bank of America, National Association	x		United States
Merrill Lynch Canada Inc.		x	United States
State Street Bank and Trust Company	x		United States
Deutsche Bank Securities Limited		x	Germany
BNP Paribas (Canada)	x		France
HSBC Bank Canada	x	x	UK
ING Bank of Canada	x		Netherlands

Source: Bank of Canada[*]

(Figure 1.4)[4]

The Bail Out numbers from Bank of Canada is even worse to get. Even going through Canadian Freedom of Information requests BOC still won't release the numbers. Though there are no numbers from BOC, but you can find detailed numbers from OFSI Office of the Superintendent of Financial Institution. They keep detailed numbers of the Canadian banks' balance sheets. And through experts at Canadian Center for Policy Alterna-

---

[3] McDonald, David. The Big Bank's Big Secret. Report. April 12, 2012.Accessed February 16, 2016.
https://www.policyalternatives.ca/sites/default/files/uploads/publicatio
ns/National%20Office/2012/04/Big%20Banks%20Big%20Secret.pdf .
[4]Ibid

tives they have managed to give us an estimated number on how much money the Central Bank gave to the Canadian banks on the FED and TARP bail out. Above are the estimated numbers of how much money Canadian banks had to take from BOC. The total amount of money utilized was about $41B. (Figure 1.4)

Participants at the Bank of Canada's bank programs had to be either Primary Dealers of Government of Canada's bonds/treasury bills or be part of the Large Value Transfer System (LVTS). The chart above outlines all the banks and financial institutions that would have access to these supports.

Estimated Utilization of CMHC Programs ($ Billions)

	Total Mortgages Sold as of Final Auction (March 24", 2010)
TD Bank	$21.9
RBC	$14.7
CIBC	$11.8
Scotiabank	$9.0
BMO	$6.7

Source: Estimates based on the financial statements of CIBC, BMO, RBC, Scotiabank, TD Bank

(Figure 1.5)[5]

The federal government also extended cash injections to Canada's big banks through CMHC's Insured Mortgage Purchase Program (IMPP). This program was by far the largest in terms of support with just over $69 billion in mortgages purchased from Canada's banks. CMHC was not providing loans that needed to be paid back, as it was the case with the other two aiding programs. CMHC was buying mortgages and, as such, the banks did not need to pay this money back. The CMHC

---

[5]Ibid

program was thus a straight cash infusion for Canada's banks. CMHC was left to decide what they will do with $69 billion worth of mortgages. In the same way that the Bank of Canada loan programs mirrored those of the U.S. Federal Reserve, the CMHC program resembled the U.S. Troubled Asset Relief Program (TARP).

Is your money safe in the banks?

CHAPTER 2

Bail INS; When a Bank Takes Your Money

Before we get into the so-called safe deposits you should know that the Government of Canada has prepared legislation to take care of any bank failures. We are not talking about bank Bail Outs, now we are talking about bail-ins or haircuts as the governments like to refer to them as or a tax. It sounds more humane than deposit confiscation to save an overleveraged failing bank, which couldn't care less about your deposits in the first place.

I've spoken to lots of Canadians that have no clue that this strategy is set and a Cyprus-style "Saving a Failing Bank" is ready to take place at any time it might be needed to keep the failing banking system alive and help bankers take home their commission checks.

If you are not aware of this legislation, here is a quick exert from the legislation that should send chills down your spine.

The Government proposes to implement a bail-in regime for systemically important banks. This regime will be designed to ensure that in the unlikely event that a systemically important bank depletes its capital, the bank can be recapitalized and returned to viability through the very rapid conversion of certain bank liabilities into regulatory capital. This will reduce risks for taxpayers. The Government will consult stakeholders on the best way to implement a bail-in regime in Canada. Implementation timelines will allow for a smooth transition for affected institutions, investors and other market participants. Systemically important banks will continually be subject to existing risk management requirements, including enhanced supervision, recovery and resolution plans. This risk management framework will limit the unfair advantage that could be gained by Canada's systemically important banks through the mistaken belief by investors and other market participants that these institutions are "too big to fail"[6]

Of course, this 3-year-old policy has now entered 3rd year of budget implementation with the latest Trudeau government in 2016.

The banks are ready to take your deposits, but how about the depositor's insurance? Isn't it supposed to protect savers up to $100k? Maybe you should think again?

---

[6] Canada. ECONOMIC ACTION PLAN 2013. By James M. Flaherty, P.C., M.P. March 21, 2013. Accessed February 25, 2016. http://www.budget.gc.ca/2013/doc/plan/budget2013-eng.pdf.

RENEWING FINANCIAL SECTOR LEGISLATION

The federal financial institutions statutes contain sunset provisions mandating renewal of banking and insurance legislation by Parliament every five years, providing an opportunity to examine the legislative and regulatory framework in light of emerging trends and developments, to ensure it remains robust and technically sound.

The Department of Finance will undertake a financial sector legislative review and begin consulting stakeholders in the coming months. To support the review, Budget 2016 proposes to provide the Department of Finance with $4.2 million over five years, starting in 2016–17, and to extend the current statutory sunset date by two years to March 29, 2019.

INTRODUCING A BANK RECAPITALIZATION "BAIL-IN" REGIME

To protect Canadian taxpayers in the unlikely event of a large bank failure, the Government is proposing to implement a bail-in regime that would reinforce that bank shareholders and creditors are responsible for the bank's risks—not taxpayers. This would allow authorities to convert eligible long-term debt of a failing systemically important bank into common shares to recapitalize the bank and allow it to remain open and operating. Such a measure is in line with international efforts to address the potential risks to the financial system and broader economy of institutions perceived as "too-big-to-fail".

The Government is proposing to introduce framework legislation for the regime along with accompanying enhancements to Canada's bank resolution toolkit. Regulations and guidelines setting out further features of the regime will follow. This will provide stakeholders with an additional opportunity to comment on elements of the proposed regime.

Bail-in Regime for Banks

Canada's financial system performed well during the 2008 global financial crisis. Since that time, Canada has been an active participant in the G20's financial sector reform agenda aimed at addressing the factors that contributed to the crisis. This includes international efforts to address the potential risks to the financial system and broader economy of institutions perceived as "too-big-to-fail". Implementation of a bail-in regime for Canada's domestic systemically important banks would strengthen our bank resolution toolkit so that it remains consistent with best practices of peer jurisdictions and international standards endorsed by the G20.

(Figure 2.0)[7]

---

[7] Canada. Department of finance. Growing the middle class budget 2016. By William Francis Morneau, P.C., M.P. 223 . March 22, 2016. Accessed June 2, 2016. http://www.budget.gc.ca/2013/doc/plan/budget2013-eng.pdf .

CHAPTER 3

Deposit Insurance Fraud, Cashless Society and Negative Interest Rates

In Canada, the CDIC Canada Deposit Insurance Corporation ought to be the insurer of bank deposits of $100k and lower. How well protected are these $100k and lower bank accounts? If we had a full-fledged destruction of the Canadian banking system and the big 5 were on the cusp of massive failure, could the CDIC cover the losses of millions of Canadians who think their bank deposits are safe with their bank?

The CDIC has over $622B+ deposits that are eligible for coverage, but only a mere $2.22B is in the fund pool to cover any of those losses. That is only 0.39% coverage of the total deposits eligible for their insurance. They might be there for minor losses, but if one of the five big banks goes under, there might be a massive shortfall. Not to worry, they can borrow up to $19B from the federal government, but the sum of $21B+ only amounts to a 3.37% coverage which isn't even close to cover one major bank failure. And if that money was taken fraudulently, you will never be able to get it back as it is not insured for fraudulent activity. The second point to also make is that these numbers are from 2012 and are now 2 years old and the number might have worsened! Here is an excerpt from the CDIC's web page.[8]

Does CDIC insure losses occurred because of fraudulent activities? CDIC is a federal Crown corporation created in 1967 to insure eligible deposits at member financial institutions in case of their failure. CDIC does not cover fraud.[9]

It is getting quite clear that they are almost lying to you as most deposits in a major failure are not insured and they are not protected from financial sector looting! Does the Central bank have any reserves to back up a failing Canadian Economy? Let's look!

The end game for the banks here in Canada seems to be a move towards a cashless society and negative interest rates. Implementing a cashless society is very important to then implement a negative interest rate. As seen in Japan, Switzerland and other negative yielding Central Bank countries where people start hoarding cash, In Switzerland businesses, people have started to take out Cash insurance. For a million Franc, they are looking at 1000 Franc insurance. If they kept this money in the bank, they would have to pay around 7500 Franc in negative interest. They saved money by putting it into a storage facility or their own personal storage instead of keeping the money in the bank. Or how about the surge in safe purchases in Japan after their central bank moved to a 0.1% negative rate. People do not want to spend their money as they have very little of it in the first place.

---

[8] Source CDIC webpage: http://www.cdic.ca/en/about-cdic/Pages/default.aspx
[9] Ibid

People keep their hard-earned money away from negative yielding deposit accounts.

Some say to me that there are no banks with negative yields, but this is not true. Banks have had negative yields for other banks and corporations, and now several banks like Raiffeisen Bank at Gmund am Tagernsee, Bank of Ireland and Royal Bank of Scotland now charge certain depositors a negative interest rate for money the people deposited in their deposit account, lending it to the bank.

So seeing this, the central planners around the world are scrambling to find ways to ban cash, to remove it from circulation and to limit the use of cash in the population like Norway, Sweden and the Eurozone too.

Some experts are calling for 2, 3 or ever 4%, even 5% negative interest rates. Well to hinder people from taking their money out in cash and stash it in their mattress there is only one thing left to do. Make the currency of the country cashless. This can be done by making it fully electronic, which in most cases is 97% of currency. This way they believe you will have to spend money.

If you do not believe that this will ever hurt Canada, then you have to rethink. Many big economies have implemented negative interest rates and here is a quote from Stephen Poloz Canada's Central Bank governor:

Negative interest rates are the fourth unconventional monetary policy tool; all I want to cover is negative interest rates, which is something you have heard a lot more about recently. In 2009, the Bank said it couldn't cut its policy rate below 0.25 percent, because we believed that zero or negative interest rates might be incompatible with some markets, such as money market funds. This was a common view at the time.

Since then, we have seen the experience of several central banks, such as the ECB and Swiss National Bank, which have adopted negative policy interest rates. There, we've seen that financial markets have been able to adapt and continue to function. Given these and other developments, the Bank is now confident that Canadian financial markets could also function in a negative interest rate environment.

Let me pause at this point to answer an obvious question. Why would anyone ever accept a negative nominal return when they could always simply hold cash and earn a zero return? A big part of the answer is that there are costs to holding currency, particularly in large quantities, and these costs affect the lower bound. Because of the costs, which include storage, insurance and security, central banks can charge negative rates on commercial bank deposits without seeing a surge in demand for bank notes.

Last month, the Bank published a staff discussion paper that analyzes those costs and how convenient and beneficial the electronic payment is, and also reflects on the experience of other countries. We now believe that the effective lower bound for Canada's policy rate is around minus 0.5 per cent, but it could be a little higher or lower. This suggests that we have more room to manoeuvre in response to adverse shocks than we believed back in 2009. We will continue to watch the experience of other countries—the Swiss policy rate, for example, is currently minus 0.75 per cent—and we will also consider what adjustments might need to be made to the Bank's operational framework should they ever be required.

To sum up, once interest rates reach very low levels, the central bank still has meaningful tools that it can deploy in its pursuit of its inflation target: offering forward guidance to financial markets to enhance policy effectiveness, large-scale asset purchases, funding for credit, and pushing short-term interest rates below zero.[10]

Ending with that, now you can see that the bankers are preparing for this, although they say that it is only an extraordinary tool they are willing to implement it if things worsen here in Canada. How can one safeguard oneself? My opinion is that you will need to separate yourself from the Fiat monetary system. Although cash is king and you should have it at home and not in the bank. In my view, there are lots of other ways to protect your wealth.

You can store gold and silver bullion in a private vault, and stay away from Canadian Maple Leafs rounds as who knows if the banksters in Canada choose to claim it as their property since it has the head of Queen Elisabeth which I think still runs a lot of the inner workings of Canada.

You can barter, use your time as currency, use alternative currencies and create other mediums of exchange locally that can hold its value and not lose it through inflation. Just act and educate other Canadians.

---

[10] Poloz, Stephen S. "Prudent Preparation: The Evolution of Unconventional Monetary Policies." Bank of Canada. December 8, 2015. Accessed June 13, 2017. http://www.bankofcanada.ca/2015/12/prudent-preparation-evolution-unconventional-monetary-policies/.

CHAPTER 4

Central Bank Reserves; an Investment With No Exit Strategy

We hear a lot about how solid the Canadian banking system is, but how solid is the backing from their Central Planners at the Bank of Canada?

What reserves do they have on their books that could make the Canadian banking sector solid?

Here is an overview from their own webpage and it becomes apparent they are only sitting on a mountain of Papers. (Figure 4.0)

As you can see Canada has a lot of paper from US dollars to IMF's Special Drawing Rights, but the size of Canada's economy make them look like a nobody when it comes to gold reserves.

[11](Figure 4.0)

The historical low of 112k Oz or less than 0.00 tons of gold held by the Bank of Canada puts them in one of the worst places in the world when it comes to gold vs. currency supply and if countries start reverting to a gold standard, Canada will be a massive loser. Back in the late 90's and early 2000's Canada had lots of gold, almost 200 tones, the historical high was over 1000 tones, but now they have a lousy 0.000 tone. It is believed that Central Banks like the Canadian and my home country the Norway dumped gold on the market throughout the 2000's to calm the markets and prevent a run on the banks. It did help for a while, but what will these banks do to protect themselves from such future occurrence. Experts say one shall have between 5-20% of its total wealth in gold, but Canada's accumulated money supply vs. gold cannot even be measured I 0.00's%

There is a need for change because if the Canadian banking system is closely examined you will see that, it is rather a minefield placed on a peaceful path throughout the forest of strong and sound banking as they claim. The people of Canada should ask the Central Bank what is your exit strategy. Having sold investments before I

---

[11] "Official International Reserves." Bank of Canada. Accessed February 30, 2016. http://www.bankofcanada.ca/rates/related/international-reserves/./

know the big importance of knowing the exit strategy of an investment you are in. This is how you get your money back. Looking at Bank of Canada's balance sheet there are few investments other than paper derivatives and currencies. The Bank of Canada might be forced to buy stocks or bad loans outright to keep the bubble up and running to make people feel "rich". The Quantitative Easing QE program might be around the corner with negative interest rates and is about to be pulled out as ammo to fight the depression gathering steam in Canada. These strategies are well used by Bank of Japan and the European Central Bank. No Central Bank if any should do nothing else than print the currency of a nation. Meddling and manipulating markets will only end up in total nationalization of corporations as the Central Bank through stock and bond purchases will end up owning anything of value.

Let's look at one of the weaknesses and what I believe is madness when a country could borrow directly from their central bank at next to nothing.

CHAPTER 5

How the Canadian Government Went Full Fiat

The Canadian Government stopped borrowing money from the Central Bank in the 70's and are instead using the 5 big banks as borrowing institutions. This is madness when the government could borrow cheap currency at nearly 0% from the Bank of Canada. Instead the government borrows at rates of 2-4%, making taxpayers pay way more than they should for the racked up Canadian debt.

So, what happened around 1974? In that year, to achieve that goal, the Committee discouraged borrowing from a nation's own central bank interest-free and encouraged borrowing from private creditors.

> The Basel Committee was established by the central-bank Governors of the Group of Ten countries of the member central banks of the Bank for International Settlements (BIS), in which Canada was included. A key objective of the Committee was and is to maintain "monetary and financial stability." To achieve that goal, the Committee discouraged borrowing from a nation's own central bank

> interest-free rate and encouraged borrowing from private
> creditors, all in the name of "maintaining the stability of the
> currency."
>
> The presumption was that borrowing from a central bank
> with the power to create money on its books would inflate
> the money supply and prices. Borrowing from private cred-
> itors, on the other hand, was considered not to be inflation-
> ary, since it involved the recycling of pre-existing money.
> What the bankers did not reveal, although they had long
> known it themselves, was that private banks create the
> money they lend just as public banks do. The difference is
> simply that a publicly-owned bank returns the interest to
> the government and the community, while a privately-
> owned bank siphons the interest into its capital account, to
> be re-invested at further interest, progressively drawing
> money out of the productive economy.

Paul Hellyer also notes that lobbying by the banks
and adoption of monetarism — the idea that "markets
know best" and should be without regulation, and that
public services should be privatized — took hold.

So, around 1974, the Government of Canada began to
borrow all the monies to cover its shortfalls from the private sector at interest rate rather than creating money
through the Bank of Canada at interest-free rate. In other
words, since 1974, the Bank of Canada has not been act-
ing in the best interest of its shareholders: the people of
Canada.

To understand how ridiculous the present situation is,
consider the 1993 Auditor General of Canada report
(Section 5.41)3 which states:

> Of this, $37 billion represents the accumulated shortfall in
> meeting the cost of government programs since Confedera-
> tion. The remainder, $386 billion, represents the amount
> the government has borrowed to service the debt created by
> previous annual shortfalls.

The cost of borrowing is the third area that affects the annual deficit. In 1991-92, the interest on the debt was $41 billion. This cost of borrowing and its compounding effect has a significant impact on Canada's annual deficits. Since Confederation up to 1991-92, the federal government accumulated a net debt of $423 billion. Of this, $37 billion represents the accumulated shortfall in meeting the cost of government programs since Confederation. The remainder, $386 billion, represents the amount the government has borrowed to service the debt created by previous annual shortfalls.

In other words, out of the accumulated debt of $423 billion, the government really needed to borrow only $37 billion—accumulated over 127 years—to cover its shortfalls on real spending for goods and services. The rest of that accumulated debt was monies borrowed to service the debt, essentially, a payment of interest on interest to the private sector when the government could have created the money to cover the shortfall at an interest free rate.

In 2011, alone, Canadian taxpayers paid the private lenders an estimated $37.7 billion to service the federal debt.

According to Paul Hellyer, from 1974–1975 to 2010, Canadian taxpayers have paid one trillion, 100 billion dollars ($1,100,000,000,000) in interest on the federal debt to private lenders.

The interest cost is huge when one can use the publicly owned Bank of Canada. It is not the best idea, but it is far better than using private banks.

We need to wake up to the banker's tight grip on the Canadian Economy. The only thing that makes Canada have this infinite growth that we have seen since 2008 is the expansion of credit and most of it comes from the Fractional Reserve Banking System i.e. Private Banks.

Debt in Canada is at a record high and with 256.08% Private Debt to GDP, Canadians are getting strangled.

All that said, I want to introduce to you what I see as a fraudulent system of making money aka. Coins and notes and making money (Seigniorage [12]) on that money as a form of revenue while that same note then loses value through inflation (the increase of money supply) You are getting hit twice as our government and the Royal Canadian Mint makes money on making the money you use every day. How much money do they make? Let me show you a couple of stats from Bank of Canada and the Royal Canadian Mint. Canada made an average of 0.18% in seigniorage of GDP that accounts for in 2015 $279M every year in revenue on making money. Over the last 10 years, this number keeps increasing annually, making the income about $2.79B in total, on money made out of thin air and then having that money lose its value, about 20% over the last 10 years. Government makes big money on printing money. Here is all the information on how the Canadian government makes money on the markup from cost to "market face value" of their bank notes and coins.

Seigniorage is the revenue earned from the issue of money. Historically, this revenue accrued to the "seigneur" or ruler. In Canada today, seigniorage can be calculated as the difference between the interest the Bank of Canada earns on a portfolio of Government of Canada securities—in which it invests the total value of all banknotes in circulation—and the cost of issuing, distributing, and replacing those notes. Example, here is a simplified example of how this works, using a $20 note, which is the most commonly used denomination. If the

---

[12] "Seigniorage" Bank of Canada. March 2013. Accessed May 30, 2016. http://www.bankofcanada.ca/wp-content/uploads/2010/11/seigniorage.pdf

Bank of Canada invests the proceeds from issuing the $20 note in a government security generating 2.5 per cent interest, this note will yield $0.50 per year of interest revenue. The overall production cost of the note is about 19 cents. Given an average life of about 7.5 years for a new bank note, the production cost of the note on average is 2.5 cents per year. If average distribution expenses of about 2 cents per year are added to this, the total average annual cost of putting this note into circulation and replacing it when it's worn is approximately 4.5 cents. Thus, the Bank of Canada earns annual net revenue of about 45.5 cents for each $20 note in circulation. A Collection of seigniorage unlike the seigniorage for coins, which is generated at the time of their sale by the Royal Canadian Mint, seigniorage on bank notes is collected over a period of years, as the Bank's portfolio of government securities generates interest revenue. How is seigniorage used? There are about $64 billion in outstanding bank notes. Seigniorage varies according to prevailing interest rates and the value of outstanding note, but has ranged from $1.4 to $2.0 billion annually in recent years. After deducting the Bank's general operating expenses of about $446 million (of which spending on bank notes is approximately 48 per cent), the remainder is paid to the Receiver General for Canada. These numbers are from March 2013.

CHAPTER 6

A Heaven For Investment Funds, MER'd To Death Through Government Collusion

The way banks make money is through fees and interest. This was recently seen as the eCommerce giant Alibaba's IPO made bankers $300M. This is only one of the ways that bankers make loads of money from being money (changers) managers. The Canadian banks and investment corporations are known for some of the world highest fees on investments. There is a book written about this and if you are a Canadian you should read this book "The Naked Investor". It is an investment insider's view of the investment and banking industry.

Many mutual funds in Canada have almost double the fees as similar funds in Europe and in the US and on top of that, there are funds on funds where you pay fees twice, sometimes making fees paid as high as 7-13%

depending on the funds. This is a clear fraud, but the Canadian SEC knows how to keep the status quo for the industry by putting out legislation that is beneficial to the big corporations and destructive to small investors and businesses trying to compete with the big ones.

(Figure 6.0)[13]

In Canada, there is one company worth looking at and that is Power Corporation of Canada. This organization

---

[13] "Organization Chart." Power Corporation of Canada. Accessed May 3, 2017. https://www.powercorporation.com/en/companies/organization-chart/.

has consolidated tremendous amounts of market capital in the fund industry, owning almost 2/3's of the industry. Instead of investing in mutual funds how about buying shares in Power Corporation of Canada. Of course, that is if you are eligible.

Power Corporation of Canada works as many American multinationals. They have a revolving door between politics and their corporations, the most controversial times have been when John Rae was the Executive Vice-President, Office of the Chairman of the Executive Committee of Power Corporation of Canada. Rae is a former executive assistant to Jean Chretien, then minister of Indian Affairs. James R. Nininger, Past Chair, Corporate Director. Serves on the Board of Management of the Canada Revenue Agency.

On daily banking there are fees, on credit cards, there are 100's of fees earned on your mortgage, there are interest rates which the banks charge. Bankers have become the ruling elite class buy being money managers and making money in billions of dollars changing hands in fees and interest rates.

The way that investments in Canada are set up is to benefit the government and banks. To get in, the government and the CRA are luring you in with a tax deduction of 15% of the small sum you invest. Then you are turned over to the bankers and investment firms who suck capital through your investment and their funds and the value of your investment is falling on top of that, in the form of inflation created by the same guys. When you are ready to retire at age 71 in Canada you must start withdrawing money from your RRSP (Registered Retirement Savings Account) and it is now becoming law that you need to take your money out and pay between 20-40%+ taxes on your hard earned and saved up money. I was looking at some top performing mutual funds in Norway, and over the last 20 years they claimed to have increased by 263%. If you take away fees and this was in Norway + fees and then you add the loss from taxes when you take out the money from your pension account, you only sit with a gain of 100% well that is suddenly only a gain of 5% every year instead of what you thought a 12.5% is return a year. Numbers in the industry are much manipulated and you won't really get to see the bad fees. You only get to see a glossy one page overview showing a return on investment, but look closer and you then see that the stats are with you contributing monthly and the return is still not that great.

Here is what you are not being told about the current retirement investment system. Here is an option for you if you are starting to lose trust in the current status quo. Here's a riddle for you: How is money like water?

Take a few moments and think about it. What are your answers?

Here are a few suggestions:

- Money, like water, slips right through your fingers.

- You can't live without water and you can't live without money.

- Money and water both flow.

- Water is everywhere and money is everywhere.

Over 95% of the water on earth is in the oceans.

Where is most of the money in the world? You guessed it – in banks. BUT – and this is critical. Whose money is it that the banks control? YOURS!

Stop and think about that for a moment. Banks control most of the money in an economy and it is not their money, but yours.

If it is our money, why don't we learn to control it and benefit from that control?

As a society, we are on a path that creates wealth for governments and businesses at the expense of the well-being of individuals and families. We have relinquished our personal freedoms and allowed ourselves to become indebted to government, corporations, creditors, and manufacturers of consumer goods.

Over the last thirty to forty years, we have misplaced some of our greatest treasures. These are not physical items or collectibles. They are the economic principles, practices and tools that have built great economies in the past.

The media and mass marketing have seduced us into serving the best interests of others instead of doing what is best for ourselves and our families. Driven by these marketing messages we have opted for a gambling mentality with our money rather than a savings mentality. We have forgotten the childhood story of the tortoise and the hare. The media and the financial services industry have worked tirelessly to create this "gambling" mentality in our society and we are all suffering for it.

We need to realize that many forces are working against us and our attempts to hold onto and grow our money. The tax collectors, the banking system and most businesses derive their profit from us as individuals. Each of these entities is designed to be as profitable as possible. For them to be profitable, they must convince us to part with our dollars. And if we are not on our guard, several dollars will flow away from us to others with minimal benefit to us.

Money, like water will follow the course of least resistance. If we don't consciously direct and manage our dollars, they will simply walk away from us. It is said that money talks, It can also be said that money walks away – quietly.

As a society, we have allowed ourselves to be lured into the notion that we can have everything we want, now, if we have enough credit. Billions of dollars are spent each year convincing us to use borrowed money to buy the things that will make us happy, rich, slim, attractive, healthy, and popular. Unfortunately, we are usually left poorer and they have become wealthier. Whenever we want to purchase and finance an item, we have control over two things – whether we buy it and how we pay for it.

If, as was mentioned earlier, banks control most of the money in the world and it is not their money but ours, why don't we create our own "banking" system? If every time we want to purchase a bigger ticket item we are going to borrow money from somewhere and pay someone else for the use of their money, why don't we borrow from ourselves and pay the principal and interest back to ourselves. Instead of debt to others, why not debt to ourselves? The same amount of dollars will be spent, but where those dollars end up and who they benefit will be very different.

Banks make a fortune every year by following a very simple system. They take in our money, they "mark it up", they lend it out to us, we pay back principal and interest and their wealth grows.

There are only four players needed to make the banking system function well:

- **A saver:** Someone needs to deposit money into the bank.
- **A borrower:** Someone wants or needs to borrow money.
- **A loan officer:** His or her job is to lend the money out as quickly as possible.
- **The bank owners:** They collect the principal and interest and take collateral to make sure they have very little risk in this venture.

Now, if the bank is using our money to perform this function (remember, they don't have any of their own money, it is our money they are using), why don't we create our own banking system? Their system is quite simple and there is a way for us to duplicate it.

The most effective way to set up your own banking system is to use a dividend paying whole life insurance plan. This is the financial tool or vehicle which allows us to mimic the banking system more closely.

So, how can dividend paying whole life insurance allow us to mimic the banking system?

Remember from above that the banking system needs four players to make their system function well – a saver, a borrower, a loan officer, and the bank owner. In a dividend paying whole life insurance plan, you are all those players.

You are the saver. As you contribute to your plan, a portion goes to pay for the death benefit and a portion goes into your cash value or savings plan. As soon as you make your first premium payment, you have created two banks within your policy. The death benefit bank is full right away. The insurance company guarantees that in case of death, the death benefit bank will be paid out to your beneficiaries so that they are well looked after. The other bank is your cash value bank. This is the portion that will increase in value every year and can grow over time to be a large tax efficient pool of money to work and retire with.

You are the borrower. Whenever you need money to finance a purchase, you can use your cash value as collateral. You are not using your own cash value so you still receive interest and dividends on the entire cash value pool. This allows compounding to do its magic. You borrow from the insurance company and use your cash value and death benefit as collateral. Up to 90% of the cash value is available to you with no questions asked. This puts you in a position of strength as you can use that money for anything you choose. It is good for emergencies and opportunities.

You are the loans officer. You set the terms as to how you want to pay back the loan. Will you pay it off monthly? When you receive a bonus from work? When you have had a profitable season? This gives you a tremendous amount of flexibility and control.

You are the bank owner. As you repay the loan, the lien against your death benefit is removed. The full amount of the principal will go to someone in your family. The interest is paid to the insurance company because that is who you borrowed the money from. As you repay the loan amount, it is all recycled back into your system and the cash value pool (your money) is now available to be used again. Also, the healthier the overall insurance pool of money is, the greater the dividend that will be paid out to you as a policy owner because you are part owner of the insurance company when a mutual insurance company is used.

It is not that you are saving money by functioning this way, it is simply a matter of who is controlling the banking function in your life. If you finance your purchases through the traditional banking system, they control the entire process and all the benefits flow to them. When you control the banking function and run it through your life insurance plan, you control the process and the benefits come back to you.

How can you accomplish the above with your own dividend paying life insurance plan?

By creating your own banking system through your dividend paying life insurance plan, instead of the flow of money going to the banks, you are recycling it back to yourself.

With your life insurance plan in place, you have created a financial vehicle that will assure you of a guaranteed income and it can be structured so that you never outlive this income.

With your life insurance plan in place, you always have access to your cash values to use as you deem fit or need. Life regularly throws us curve balls and in those situations, we need access to readily available funds.

Your life insurance plan carries a death benefit and so upon your death; some of your wealth can be passed on to your children or charities in a tax-free manner.

By creating your own "banking system" using a properly structured dividend whole life insurance plan, you have taken control of your finances and you are growing your money in a safe, predictable and a tax efficient environment.

Talking about the bankers, let's look at a trend that will always destroy a currency; compounding interest and how the Canadian Monetary System is not in any way better than the American or any other centrally planned economy Monetary System.

CHAPTER 7

The Paper Bubble of Debt

The start of any paper debt bubble over the last 1000 years starts with a devaluation or debasement of the coinage of a nation. Let me quickly show you how the Roman Empire Debased their currency first and then show you throughout the last 50 years how Canada did it in a very similar manner.

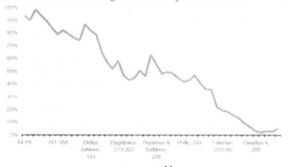

(Figure 7.0)[14]

---

[14]"http://www.zerohedge.com/sites/default/files/images/user5/imageroot/images/Silver%20content.jpg. Accessed May 12, 2017.

The Chart above shows the decrease of silver content in the Roman Denarius over the time span of 2 centuries. After Emperor Claudius II, they started to use copper coinage and the debasement and destruction of Roman wealth became full circle.

Canada has taken a very similar approach, but in a faster manner. We have in today's technological era about 97% of all money electronically, but the remaining coinage has been debased quite rapidly since the late 60's. Here is an overview of how the Canadian coinage got debased.

I will use the $1 coin or as it is currently known as the loonie. Below is a historical composition of the now $1 coin called the loonie.

1935 - 1967

Composition: 80% silver, 20% copper

Weight (g): 23.3

Diameter (mm): 36.06

Thickness (mm): 2.84

1968 - 1982

Composition: 99.9% nickel

Weight (g): 15.62

Diameter (mm): 32.13

Thickness (mm): 2.62

1982 – 1986

Composition: 99% nickel (minimum)

Weight (g): 15.62

Diameter (mm): 32.13

Thickness (mm): 2.55

1987–2011

Composition: 91.5% Ni,

8.5% bronze plating

(88% Cu, 12% Sn)

2007–2011

Some coins used brass plating instead

2012–

99.9% steel, brass plating

Today 1 Canadian 1962 Dollar equals $22

Today 1 Canadian 2015 Dollar equals 15c[15]

---

[15] Numbers from Royal Canadian Mint. Accessed April 29, 2017.

(Figure 7.1)[16]

M0 is a measure of the money supply which combines any liquid or cash assets held within a central bank and the amount of physical currency circulating in the economy. In the United Kingdom, the M0 supply is also referred to as narrow money.

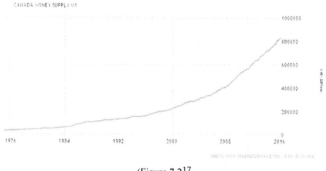

(Figure 7.2[17]

M1 is a metric for the money supply of a country and includes physical money — paper and coin — as well as checking accounts, demand deposits and negotiable order of withdrawal (NOW) accounts. The most liquid por-

---

[16] http://www.tradingeconomics.com. Accessed December 19, 2016.
[17] Ibid

tions of the money supply are measured by M1 because it contains currency and assets that can be converted to cash quickly. "Near money" and "near, near money," which fall under M2 and M3, cannot be quickly converted to currency.

Using M1 as the definition of a country's money supply, it references money as a medium of exchange, with demand deposits and checking accounts as the most commonly used exchange mediums following the development of debit cards and ATMs. Of all the components of the money supply, M1 is defined has the most narrow. It doesn't include financial assets like savings accounts. It is the money supply metric most frequently utilized by economists to reference how much money is in circulation in a country.

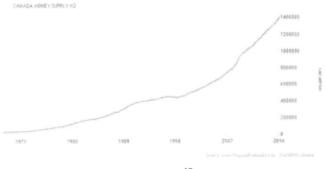

(Figure 7.3)[18]

M2 is a measure of the money supply that includes all elements of M1 as well as "near money." M1 includes cash and checking deposits, while near money refers to savings deposits, money market securities, mutual funds and other time deposits. These assets are less liquid than

---

[18] Ibid

M1 and not as suitable as exchange mediums, but they can be quickly converted into cash or checking deposits.

M2 is a broader money classification than M1, because it includes assets that are highly liquid but are not cash. A consumer or business typically doesn't use savings deposits and other non-M1 components of M2 when making purchases or paying bills, but it could convert them to cash in relatively short order. M1 and M2 are closely related, and economists like to include the more broadly defined definition for M2 when discussing the money supply, because modern economies often involve transfers between different account types. For example, a business may transfer $10,000 from a money market account to its checking account. This transfer would increase M1, which doesn't include money market funds, while keeping M2 stable, since M2 contains money market accounts.

(Figure 7.4)[19]

M3 is a measure of the money supply that includes M2 as well as large time deposits, institutional money market funds, short-term repurchase agreements and other larger liquid assets. The M3 measurement includes

---

[19] Ibid

assets that are less liquid than other components of the money supply and are referred to as "near, near money," which are more closely related to the finances of larger financial institutions and corporations than to those of small businesses and individuals.

The money supply, sometimes referred to the money stock, has many different classifications with respect to liquidity, and M3 is just one of them. The total money supply includes all the currency in circulation as well as liquid financial products, such as certificates of deposit (CDs). The M3 classification is the broadest measure of an economy's money supply. It emphasizes money as a store-of-value more than being a medium of exchange — hence the inclusion of less-liquid assets in M3. It is used by economists to estimate the entire money supply within an economy, and by governments to direct policy and control inflation over the medium and long-term periods.

M3 can be thought of as a congregation of all other classifications of money (M0, M1 and M2) plus all the less liquid components of the money supply. M0 refers to the currency in circulation, such as coins and cash. M1 includes M0 plus demand deposits such as checking accounts as well as traveler's checks; M1 includes the currency that is out of circulation but is readily available. M2 includes all M1 (and all M0 as a result) plus savings deposits and certificates of deposit, which are less liquid than checking accounts. M3 includes all M2 (and all M1 and M0 as a result) but also adds the least liquid components of the money supply that are not in circulation, such as repurchase agreements that do not mature for days or weeks.

As you can clearly see that over time compounding interest borrowed against non-productive investments like credit cards, margin debt on stock market gambling gets uncontrollable, and at one moment it will be a hockey stick moment bigger than any we have ever seen. I explain money creation this way. "If I had the only $1000 in the world and you wanted to borrow them from me. I would say great, let's do it. I give you the $1000, but there is one catch. I want the $1000 back, but with interest. So you might ask. How will I be able to pay you back the interest? I would say don't worry, I will print the interest, but I also want interest back on the interest I just borrowed you, and on top of that I want more interest."

It gets clearer when I explain how money gets created, how the above charts never go into a deflating trend as all currencies created has an interest charged on it except the basic money supply; the paper and coins you use on a daily basis as cash.

I do know that there is a big difference between what I call unbacked debt and backed debt. I have no problem with a system borrowing money to someone that can pay the money back with a simple and not compound interest. And if the system was without the Fractional Reserve Banking system which I briefly explain in my first book "The End of Freedom: How Our Monetary System Enslaves Us". When you borrow money to someone who can innovate for humanity or create a business or service people want, there is nothing wrong with lending them money and then they give you a little extra back at the backend for borrowing your hard-earned wealth. Where I have, a problem is when you borrow money in the financial markets against derivatives, speculation and betting on markets. This type of borrowing that are not used to create what I explained above as real wealth, but merely creates money with money without benefitting anyone but yourself is un-backed debt and does not create any value. It is the same for the credit companies' borrowing money against houses that should depreciate and having speculators and banks pushing the price up to make more money or you going on a vacation borrowing money at 19.9% from a credit card company or you going to university taking a useless political or a social studies degree that produce nothing more but red tape. It creates bubbles as shown in the charts above and they will fail together with the failure of the monetary system itself.

Study how any form of compounding effect works and you will soon see the mathematical certainty of a hockey stick moment of destruction as this is how bacteria grows and any other species in the world will grow exponentially until we have depleted all the food and resources available. The monetary system destroys wealth in the same way rapid expansion of deer population expands till there are no more resources to carry the population and it dies off.

Interesting how laws of science and mathematics always plays out as certain forces explaining history and todays certain coming failures of monetary system's word wide and in Canada. Talking about compounding and how the monetary system needs a constant feed of people getting into debt or else it will collapse in on itself as the demand for food by the deer disappear and they die off, the money supply goes into failure mode as interest comes due on those unsustainable debt loans and when there is no more money created to pay off the interest another certainty kicks into place "Bankruptcies and foreclosures". At the top of it are the lenders who can get the asset and business back for next to nothing.

Mentioning that since November 04th 2015 we have a new prime minister in Canada named Justin Trudeau. Of course, his dad Pierre Trudeau grew the national government by almost 150%. He also started to sell off Canada's gold holding. His son Justin is set to double the Canadian National debt yet once again. Already the national Canadian debt is not repayable. With the current belief of the government being that they give people rights and when government grows it is a good thing. This idea is what has brought down many empires throughout history, which includes the French revolution and the fall of The Roman Empire. The current Canadian debt is around $636.1B from the government's own projections this number is set to double. See the table below showing the projection made by the Canadian Department of Finance.

Detailed Fiscal Projections

Table 3
Long-Term Fiscal Projections
billions of dollars

	2021–22	2025–26	2030–31	2035–36	2040–41	2045–46	2050–51	2055–56
Revenues	355.0	409.5	488.9	587.5	708.3	853.6	1,026.4	1,232.8
Program expenditures	336.5	392.2	472.1	563.1	669.0	792.8	939.3	1,112.9
Public debt charges	33.1	42.3	53.2	63.2	73.2	82.3	89.4	93.4
Budgetary balance	-14.6	-25.0	-36.4	-38.8	-33.9	-21.6	-2.2	26.5
Federal debt	746.4	826.8	992.0	1,183.8	1,366.6	1,501.6	1,554.3	1,483.5
Nominal GDP[1]	2,453.7	2,837.7	3,396.3	4,085.8	4,932.1	5,946.8	7,150.9	8,574.5

[1] On a calendar-year basis

(Figure 7.5)[20]

One thing the Canadian government need is your taxes to pay for their existence. The other problem with debt in Canada is private and I made it clear above, what kind of debt is bad and what is good. Here is Canada's bad debt.

---

[20] Update of Long-Term Economic and Fiscal Projections." Department of Finance Canada. December 23, 2016. Accessed March 03, 2017. https://www.fin.gc.ca/pub/ltefp-peblt/report-rapport-eng.asp

CHAPTER 8

Building Their Way to Prosperity?

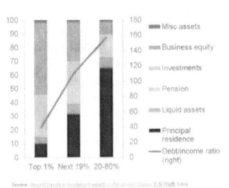

The rich hold assets, the poor have debt
Household wealth by percentile (% gross assets)

(Figure 8.0)[21]

In Canada, the Real Estate boom has seen no end. Markets like Winnipeg where I live close to haven't seen a real downturn for over 30 years+. What is one

---

[21] Levy Economics Institute

of the main drivers of the middle classes so called wealth? Real Estate, their house is looked at as an asset as it counts for 70% of the middle-class wealth. When your own residence is an asset that is when a bird becomes an elephant. Anything that you have that takes more money out of your pocket on a monthly basis than it brings in is a liability and your house end up in this category.

Real Estate booms are used to convince the public that they are becoming wealthier as more and more people are getting into real estate and getting loans for it. This creates a supply and demand issue which then drives up prices. The more this price can be driven up the better for banks and politicians as the people can now use their homes as ATM and wastefully spend the newly gained equity on vacations, cars and more doodads as Robert Kiyosaki calls them.

The Canadian economy and their GDP heavily depend on growth through real estate and the construction that the credit boom creates. A whopping 19%+ of Canada's GDP comes from real estate and construction, and here are the latest numbers shown in a chart.

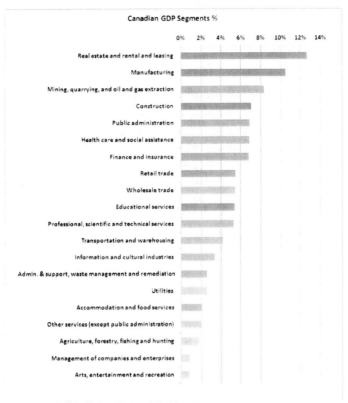

(Figure 8.1)[22]

Something is wrong when 1/5 of your economy is dependent on continuous building of new homes, condos, business and industrial real estate. The biggest growth is in Residential and that is the problem. The real economy of production and commodities are not there. Rather, profit driven investments in real estate which in many cases gives no real value back to the community and are driven by cheap money from the central bankers. Mean-

---

[22] "The Canadian Economy at a Glance." InvestorsFriend. November 03, 2007. Accessed May 10, 2016. http://www.investorsfriend.com/canadian-gdp-canadian-imports-and-exports/.

while the middle class think they are getting richer. Cheap money creates massive distortions and great leverage that could only end one way "bad", as people want to exit.

The biggest risk markets currently are Vancouver who were driven by the mass influx of Chinese investors and of course the low interest rate environment created by the Bank of Canada trying to boost housing prices to avert a recession. Let's not forget the number two which is Toronto. These markets have seen a massive influx of cheap capital from what Vancouver has seen.

Chart 9: **Regional divergence in house price growth partly reflects employment growth**

6-month average of year-over-year growth rates

(Figure 8.2)[23]

23 "Financial System Review" Bank of Canada June 2016. Accessed April 05, 2017. http://www.bankofcanada.ca/wp-content/uploads/2016/06/fsr-june2016.pdf

It is a way for the banks to reap great profits through all the fees, interest and long term low risk as they own the house until you pay the last penny on your mortgage.

I am not saying that Real Estate is a bad investment as a matter of fact, if you know what you are doing you can play these markets, but you need to understand this one fundamental misconception the public has about their own home. It is not an asset until you sell it off or rent it out for a positive cash flow. Assets bring in real cash flow. Next time someone list your house with a mortgage on it, know that it is a liability until you start making more money on it in a month than you pay in expenses.

Talking about Real Estate and the main driving force behind it we are going to look at debt the driver of almost all money. Money = Debt as most money created is created as debt through the banking system or through Corporate and Sovereign Debt (Bonds). Only a little fraction is money without debt, which is "Cash".

Do you believe these stats affect the Canadian economy's future in a bad way?

I believe that, most especially the Bank of Canada's Reserves is an issue that should be spoken about on a daily basis as Canada is one of the worst positioned G20 countries as they have 0.00% Gold Reserves to GDP compared to Russia, Europa and the US at 2.2% to 2.7%. A move to a gold standard would devastate the Canadian economy. Canadian banking fees are the highest in the world and the organizations running this crime syndicate do not want any competition as they use the Securities to try to shut down or make it hard for any competition that may arise.

Canada's Money supply is still booming together with almost all the other 40+ economies I track on a quarterly basis. Real Estate's exponential growth in many places in Canada, especially in Vancouver and Toronto is also a worrisome signal as these booms are fueled by debt bubbles.

As a last update before this book gets published I would like to give you information on something that is worrisome for the Canadian banking system and the real estate markets, especially with the newest development as of April 17th 2017[24] that seems to be the start of a derivative based mortgage bundling system with BMO bundling $2B of "prime" mortgages into something called a mortgage backed security. Supposedly 95% of the mortgages have a rating of AAA (Prime) which is the same grade as the Canadian Government. The Canadian Government can print money to pay their debt. The people who have these mortgages do not have the possibility to print money out of thin air if they lose their job. In the same Mortgage Backed Security issue there are also B2 rated mortgages, which are (Highly Speculative) and there is also non-rated investment in the derivative issue from BMO. The main question is, can we trust Moody's to rate these investment mortgages better than they did in 2005-2008 when they, Standard and Poor's were caught in their rating scheme lying about the true rating of the underlying mortgages that blew up in 2007[25].

You have to start wondering how great this will be when proud bankers like Richard Hunt, an analyst at Moody's Investors Service who rated the deal, "Canada's is one of the few jurisdictions that doesn't have a devel-

---

[24] McNeely, Allison. "BMO Bundles Uninsured Mortgages in a Canadian Bond First." Bloomberg.com. April 17, 2017. Accessed May 20, 2017.
https://www.bloomberg.com/news/articles/2017-04-17/bank-of-montreal-to-offer-mbs-as-canada-shrinks-mortgage-support?cmpId=flipboard.

[25] "Subprime mortgage crisis." Wikipedia. Accessed June 15, 2017.
https://en.wikipedia.org/wiki/Subprime_mortgage_crisis.

oped RMBS market, this could be the first step to getting that done." MBS have not done too well as the central banks like the US Federal Reserve holds almost $1.78T USD[26] in bad derivatives on their books bought from the banks as they needed to avoid failures. All I can say is that this new development looks very much like a bank trying to push bad debt off their balance sheet and pass it on to investors like pension funds and others who can only invest in Prime rated investments.

(Figure 8.3)[27]

Breaking: As I am getting ready to publish this book, it's clear evidence of a massive real estate bubble about to burst. The news as of 27th of April 2017 a Home Capital Group one of Canada's biggest mortgage lenders share is down to almost 61% as it got an emergency loan arrangement for a $2 billion credit line to counter evapo-

---

[26] https://markets.newyorkfed.org/soma/download/739/mbs?client=GUI. Accessed May 22, 2017.

[27] Google Stock Prices. Accessed April 27, 2017.

rating deposits at terms that will leave the alternative mortgage lender unable to meet financial targets, and to worsen the case it may leave it insolvent in a very short notice.

Translated: wait until last night's depositor bank jog suddenly becomes a sprint.

The loan will provide Home Capital with more than C$3.5 billion in total funding, more than twice the C$1.5 billion in liquid assets it held as of April 24. It also has $200 million in securities available for sale, and high interest savings account balances fell about 25% to $1.4 billion over the past month. Home Capital relies on deposits to fund their mortgage loans; following today's announcement the company's liquidity is certain to get even worse as all non-distressed sources of cash are pulled.

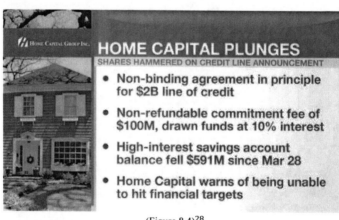

(Figure 8.4)[28]

---

[28] "Canada's Housing Bubble Explodes As Its Biggest Alternative Mortgage Lender Crashes Most In History." ZeroHedge. April 25, 2017. Accessed April 26, 2017. http://www.zerohedge.com/news/2017-04-26/canadas-housing-bubble-explodes-its-biggest-mortgage-lender-crashes-most-history.

The Home Capital group used to be investment grade, but their credit ratings were a huge miscalculation. This was done by the rating agencies.

Another warning came from Canada's Fannie Mae. The CMHC, they insure subprime loans. They did an overview of Canada's current real estate market and found this result.

(Figure 8.5)[29]

[29] "Strong evidence of overall problematic conditions despite some housing markets showing signs of improvement." CMHC. April 25, 2017. Accessed April 26,

When I compare the current situation to the time I started writing this book in early 2016, things have changed rapidly as Canada's debt crisis worsen. It is starting to unravel as I predicted earlier in my book. This will only cause more hardships and a deflation which will entail more inflation and currency printing through Quantitative Easing (QE) from the Bank of Canada and the Canadian Government who will continue to run deficits. Be prepared for a major correction, not just in housing debt, but in all Canadian's debt. The housing market is only one of the big debt bubbles in Canada.

2017. https://www.cmhc-schl.gc.ca/en/corp/nero/nere/2017/2017-04-26-1200.cfm?utm_source=twitter-main&utm_medium=link&utm_campaign=mac#mediaDownload.

CHAPTER 9

The Canadian Debt Addiction

Debt is the mother of all indicators of a healthy system. When debt rises rapidly and other indicators like unemployment and Business Start-ups vs. bankruptcies rises. Something is wrong when people need to get into debt to afford goods, services and shelter. As the US and many other countries who suffer have had a minor rise of private debt, Canada has had an explosion. Canadians lend more than ever as they anticipate good times ahead. Their houses are their ATM's and Credit is cheap through car loans and credit cards.

Canadians have more debt load now than ever before in the history of the country and it is not slowing down. Here are some charts to show how Canadians have gotten more and more into debt since 2008.

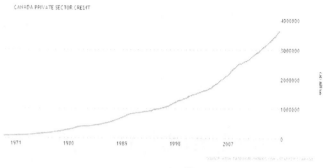

(Figure 9.0)[30]

(Figure 9.1)[31]

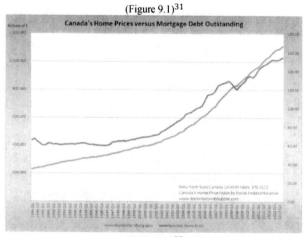

(Figure 9.2)[32]

---

[30] http://www.tradingeconomics.com. Accessed June 30, 2016.
[31] Ibid

The statistics shows that Canada's ratio of household credit market debt to disposable income increased to a new level of 163.4 per cent in the second quarter compared with 162.1 per cent in the first three months of 2016.That means Canadians owe just over $1.63 for every $1 in disposable income they earn in a year.

The number below shows a total private debt to GDP. This is how much debt is borrowed by private people and businesses. The number is quite mind numbing and as of recent, it currently stands at 256.08%. THIS IS ONE OF THE HIGHEST IN THE WORLD

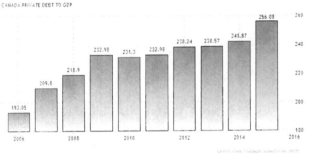

(Figure 9.4)[33]

One of the main reasons for this high private debt is taxes. It is of course my point of view and economists might disagree, but I will show you the top privately indebted countries below and you can easily see many of the highest taxed countries are at the top of this list:

---

[32] Stats Canada. Accessed May 25, 2016.

[33] http://www.tradingeconomics.com

Country	Last		Previous	Highest	Lowest		
1. **Luxembourg**	494.45	Dec/15	466	497	262	%	Yearly
2. **Ireland**	421.94	Dec/15	401	422	189	%	Yearly
3. **Iceland**	323.51	Dec/15	380	380	273	%	Yearly
4. **Norway**	278.69	Dec/15	270	279	195	%	Yearly
5. **Portugal**	275.29	Dec/15	293	315	149	%	Yearly
6. **Sweden**	269.85	Dec/15	270	275	187	%	Yearly
7. **Netherlands**	266.14	Dec/15	269	276	248	%	Yearly
8. **Belgium**	258.20	Dec/15	254	258	150	%	Yearly
9. **Denmark**	257.12	Dec/15	268	286	189	%	Yearly
10. **Canada**	256.08	Dec/15	242	256	177	%	Yearly

(Figure 9.5)[34]

Countries like Norway, Sweden and Denmark are relatively high on this chart. It's not a surprise that the level of debt is closely correlated with the level of government. The top 10 for Government expenditure as a part of GDP has a lot of common names on it. When people get taxed and fried to death by their governments. The only way to afford nice things is to get into debt. With the younger generation getting into debt as well with Canada's current student loan level being at $16.53B there is no doubt that this debt bubble is creating more inflation and higher prices every year. The more people get into debt and the higher the debt burden the less we can afford. Also the increased debt out of nothing has increased the same supply of things related to prices

---

[34] ibid

normally rises every year leaving people with less and less money in their pockets.

The end game is a debt collapse and a potential hyper-inflation of the Canadian dollar as Central Bankers in Canada believe in printing currency to fix this issue which will only make things a lot worse.

As you can see from the last chart above, Canadian household debt is skyrocketing while it's deflating all over the world. Making Canada look like everything is great. The truth is that Canadians live in a mirage of a recovery as the pump and dump of debt by the private banks have helped to increase the bubble which should have crashed in 2008. Cheap currency has helped to keep the status quo, instead of raising incomes for people. The bankers have forced Canadians to accumulated debt to keep the inflation gap from eating them alive as they have less and less money.

Debt is money and Money is Debt in today's system, when debt disappears so does money. Can Canadian debt continue to increase or will it hit the wall as the maximum number of debtors and the possible payback of the debt has hit the maximum possible potential? And will it then hit a mass bankruptcy and foreclosures because there are no more people that have the possibility or willingness to get into more debt to pay off the interest on the current debt. In a Ponzi scheme, you always need new blood at the bottom to feed the top and when no more money is created to pay off the racked up debt by the top of the pyramid. There will be no more money to pay off the interest that doesn't exist in money yet.

Debt is dangerous and it has destroyed many empires throughout the last 2000+ years a FIAT Currency system is a Ponzi scheme by design and we all know what happens to them when no more people will participate as the Ponzi scheme is discovered.

Something that is helping Canada, especially in the Central and Western provinces is the real economy of commodities. How big is the commodity economy in Canada?

CHAPTER 10

Gold and Commodities; Can It Save the Canadian Economy?

While money gets created, where is the possibility to preserve wealth and keep wealth? What goes up in price if I may ask? Food, Metals and other consumer goods have gone up in price ever since we moved from controlling the monetary supply to the start up of a central bank in 1914.

Can Farming and commodities keep the economy alive or will the debt burden be too big? Commodities and Food are very important as we rely on them to survive in our daily life. What would the world be today without Silver? We wouldn't have Solar Power, Electronics or Cars as they all have an amount of Silver content that they couldn't exist without. How about water? The most important commodity for survival of the human species is water and food. Can we make sure to keep the food and commodities needed so that in a case of crisis we don't have to worry as we are self-sufficient? If the Supermarket does not get supplies it takes on an average 3 days to run out of supplies in a city. For survival and general protection against fiat currencies it would be great to have some food, water and other commodity reserves as they might be too expensive or in short supply.

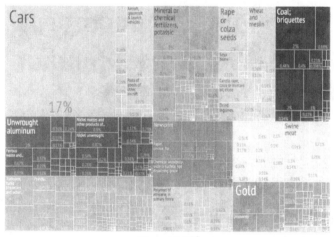

(Figure 10.0)[35]

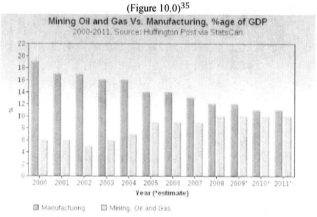

35 "Economy of Canada." Wikipedia. Accessed June 23, 2016. https://en.wikipedia.org/wiki/Economy_of_Canada.

(Figure 10.1)[36]

The Central and Western Economies of Canada do have a bigger influence of Commodities and agriculture, but unfortunately the Real Estate and Finance Sectors are exploding while the Commodity, Agricultural and Energy sectors are slowing down as the fiat currency system is making its last cycle of decadence and spending on things that do not count in real economic terms. Things extracted from the earth and harvested are real and they usually benefit people. Oil exploration in Canada is an example of how a very expensive way of extracting oil was made possible by cheap money and high oil prices.

Oil is one of the biggest exports of Central Canada, but it is dependent on the US not producing more oil. Canada is very dependent on the US to Export their commodities and Food. Over 70% of their total export goes to the US so the continuous bad economy in the US is not helping to grow the real economic sectors of Canada and is forcing people into the Real Estate and Financial Sectors.

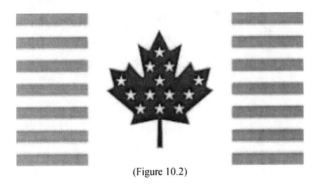

(Figure 10.2)

---

[36] Stats Canada. Accessed December 10, 2016.

Can the commodities sector help Canada stay afloat when the Debt bubble pops? Certain Provinces in the West can be more self-sufficient, but the financialization and the move away from the real economy can do more harm than good to the economy.

A brief history of Canada's gold

Canada used to have a big amount of gold in their possession at the Bank of Canada. But what has happened over the last 66 years? I want to share with you what Canada did with their Gold holdings since 1950. Below is an array of statistics brought from different reports on Central Bank holdings of gold.

GOLD RESERVES 1950-2016

SELECTED COUNTRIES all figures in metric tonnes fine gold

1950: 515 1951: 748 1952: 786 1953: 876
1954: 954 1955: 1008 1956: 980 1957: 978
1958: 958 1959: 853 1960: 787 1961: 841
1962: 630 1963: 726 1964: 912 1965: 1023
1966: 929 1967: 902 1968: 767 1969: 775
1970: 703 1971: 706 1972: 683 1973: 683
1974: 683 1975: 683 1976: 672 1977: 684
1978: 688 1979: 690 1980: 653 1981: 636
1982: 630 1983: 627 1984: 626 1985: 625
1986: 613 1987: 576 1988: 533 1989: 501
1990: 459 1991: 403 1992: 309 1993: 188
1994: 121 1995: 106 1996: 96 1997: 96

1998:77 2000: 38.7 2001: 32.7 2002: 18.6
2003: 3.4 2004: 3.4 2005: 3.4 2006: 3.4
2007: 3.4 2008: 3.4 2009: 3.4 2010: 3.4
2011: 3.4 2012: 3.4 2013: 3 2014: 3 2015:
1.7 2016: 0[37]

As you can see from the above stats gold has played an important role as a reserve asset for the Central Bank of Canada, but what has happened is that the Keynesian economics kicked in after the 60's. The highest gold holdings were in 1965 as highlighted above. The belief that gold has no intrinsic value and that debt creation and government spending is the way to go. The problem is that Canada's debt levels and government deficits are spiraling out of control. The belief is that the government just needs to create more money and create inflation, so that the debt that they had before becomes less worth and they can pay it back with the new debt. The problem here comes when they finally tell the citizens of Canada that they can never pay back their debt and they must print so rapidly that the value of Canadian dollars will fall so fast that the inflation spikes and might cause a hyperinflation or a debt collapse and default of the Canadian government.

For those who believe that this debt creation scheme can go on forever, I must say that they are wrong. There are over 100 currencies that failed just in the 1900's. This has of course different causes, but the main idea behind it was the idea of a nation, forcing its paper monetary system onto the population making it illegal to use other forms of payment. But this will change as the system collapses on itself and we need to prepare for what is

---

[37] World Goal council. Accessed December 12, 2016.

coming next. History can repeat itself and the Canadian Fiat Dollar has no different endgame than a collapse of its value in its current monetary state. We will see a blossom of the use of Gold and Silver. In Canada, the banking sectors have a strangle hold on the people in a way that no one really understands how gold and silver works. Gold and Silver is money. The campaign against the barbarous relics have been good, but people are waking up and I believe Canadians will at one point understand how important it is to have something that can hold its value through a structural crisis in the coming systemic issues that the fiat currency system has.

Canada has gold within their borders and I think we as Canadian's should protect ourselves with this asset to make sure they are not pulled down the paper trail and lose our valuable assets as the Canadian Dollar fails.

I have been talking about the importance of Commodities and the lack of an understanding among people on how gold and silver is just as important as insurance. There are other dangers lurking in the Canadian financial wilderness and one of the most devastating ones is the CRA, which is not part of the government, but it is a crown corporation. Like the Chinese State owned Enterprise's, the Crown Corporations have benefited from the government's easy access to lobbying policy changes to help them thrive more and destroy the private businesses.

CHAPTER 11

Tax Collection; a Profitable Business

The CRA or Canada Revenue Agency is not run by the government, but rather for a non-profit organization that has a mission to collect as much taxes as possible on the behalf of the government. The CRA has been caught numerous times without numbers using scare tactics to almost extort money from individuals, in which they were not supposed to pay, but they will tell you that you need to pay your taxes before you hire a good accountant to help you mitigate or even get money back on what the CRA said you owed them and had to pay.

Here are a couple of Cases where the CRA overpower and take advantage of people:

http://www.huffingtonpost.ca/karen-selick/cra-illegal-taxes_b_3804989.html

http://www.thebottomlinenews.ca/index.php?section=article&articleid=547

http://www.thor.ca/blog/2013/06/cra-loses-another-s-231-2-third-party-requirement-case/

http://www.productionheads.com/2009/02/335/

http://www.huffingtonpost.ca/georgialee-lang/hal-neumann-cra-case-appeal_b_893627.html

http://www.newsoptimist.ca/article/20140812/BATTLEFORD0304/308129999/-1/battleford/revenue-agency-loses-battle-but-continues-to-harass-taxpayer

The official mission statement of the CRA is "to administer tax, benefits, and related programs, and to ensure compliance on behalf of governments across Canada, thereby contributing to the ongoing economic and social well-being of Canadians." For the CRA, compliance means filing tax returns by the deadline, ensuring the declaration is complete and true, and paying the Canadian government what the CRA has determined is due in a timely fashion.

The CRA has become a destructive force and so has most other tax collectors for other countries. The most notorious ones are the IRS in the US having their own SWAT teams to raid people's businesses and homes if they believe you have hidden some tax dollars from them. When you give too much power to anyone there will be people seeking to get into those roles of power to misuse them for their own good. It is just human nature and many government institutions create positions like this on default by creating auditors, inspectors and semi police. These regulations of tax collection are not new and they were dated as far back as the dark ages when you had to pay taxes directly to the King when his tax collectors came and knocked on your door.

(Figure 11.0)

The *Income War Tax Act, 1917*, received Royal Assent on September 20, 1917. The scheme of the legislation provided for a simple and accessible appeals procedure, but not one without hazard to the taxpayer. Taxes were to be paid within one month from the date of mailing of the notice of assessment. Any objection to the assessment was to be made personally or by an agent (not necessarily a solicitor), in writing and in a form prescribed by the Act to the Minister of Finance within 20 days after the mailing of the notice of assessment. Failing that, the right to appeal was lost, unless the Minister exercised his discretion to extend the appeal period.[38]

---

[38] "Tax Court of Canada." About the Court - Full History. Accessed July 11, 2016. http://cas-ncr-nter03.cas-satj.gc.ca/portal/page/portal/tcc-cci_Eng/About/Full_history.

Taxes only become necessary to keep up a big government/empire. As they grow bigger and bigger, they need to steal more and more money from the productive group of society to pay themselves. The only income the Government has comes from taxes. And when government gets too big it will become a self-destructive force as it passes over 51% of the total economy.

What then happens is that, there is not enough income from taxes in the private sector and they will decline into oblivion as they can't afford to pay themselves and will need to print money to get out of it which will only destroy the economy further as the rentier class emerges using money to make money! The income tax acts of both the US and Canada came about from removing productive people from the society and sending them to war to destroy wealth and they had to get paid and there was no tax on people's income so the government came up with a "fantastic idea" of taxing your hard-earned money.

Almost a century later the warnings of those who studied history that said the income tax might start at 1%, but history shows that the tax rate will go up to 50%-60%. This person was made fun of as people said why do you think that would happen? Well, who is laughing today? Taxes will only increase and so will government until the system collapses on itself. That brings us to the last point and that is CPP; the Canadian Pension Plan.

Talking about things that collapse which the government's deficit spending does, the CPP will be a great example of something that worked when there were more workers than retirees.

I talked in this post about Canada's debt, which is ever increasing. The debt burden on today's Fractional Reserve Banking system will only increase as the newly created debt will always have interest charged on it, and that interest does not exist. If we pay off all our debt, there would still be interest owed. And the system would collapse. Today's system is built just like a Ponzi scheme and if there are no new borrowers of money to borrow more money to pay off the already due interest the loans will fail and the system will contract as the Ponzi scheme falls in on itself, but after this happens the banksters are still in control its just you that's lost everything you owned because you had taken out loans from your bank.

We also wrote about how Commodities play an important role in the Canadian economy when the system collapses. As Wealth or owned commodities will always have a real value that will never really go down in value as the supply of paper currency is the only thing that fluctuates. It is not all of Canada that is commodity rich, but the Western parts of Canada are witnessing some growth while the big financial centers are slow. The Western provinces sit on a lot of commodities and Agricultural land. When debt and money creation skyrockets having land that is in good condition or having access to commodities becomes an important survival mechanism to the paper apocalypse that is slowly moving towards us. But do remember that of all of Canada's exports 75%+ goes to our neighbours south and if their economy slows or crashes so do ours!

We also discussed the CRA, Canada Revenue Agency and how they are used as an enforcer for the government mafia to take in taxes on behalf of the government. Since the early 1900's when the income tax code came into existence the Canadian tax code was just one page.

Unlike the United Kingdom and the United States, Canada avoided charging an income tax prior to the First

World War. The lack of income tax was a key component in Canada's efforts to attract immigrants as Canada offered a lower tax regime compared to almost every other country. Prior to the war, Canadian federal governments relied on tariffs and customs income under the auspices of the National Policy for most of their revenue, while the provincial governments sustained themselves primarily through their management of natural resources (the Prairie provinces being paid subsidies by the federal government as Ottawa retained control of their natural resources for the time being). The federal Liberal Party considered the need to introduce an income tax should their negotiation of a free trade agreement with the United States in the early 20th century succeed, but the Conservatives defeated the Liberals in 1911 over their support of free trade. The Conservatives opposed income tax as they wanted to attract immigrants, primarily from the United Kingdom and the United States, and they wanted to give immigrants some incentive to come to Canada.

Wartime expenses forced the Tories to re-consider their options and in 1917, the wartime government under Sir Robert Borden, imposed a "temporary" income tax to cover expenses. Despite the new tax the Canadian government ran up considerable debts during the war and were unable to forego income tax revenue after the war ended. With the election of the Liberal government of Prime Minister William Lyon Mackenzie King, much of the National Policy was dismantled and income tax has remained in place ever since.

You can see from this that taxes were almost non-existent, but as government grew and grew the few percent, for example the income tax has now increased into double digit. When the income tax was created in the US some congressmen warned that the tax would end up becoming as high as 30-50%. They were laughed at, but who is laughing today when income tax in the highest brackets are way above that and the government has 100's of more tax regulations. What happened? As the governments continue to grow, unless we the people interfere there will be even higher taxes. Now your savings looks like it's becoming the next victim of big bank and greedy government attributing to the case. The chase of accruing ultimate power is a result of greed in every empire throughout history.

To end it, I will show you a CRA's business entry in Bloomberg's research on privately owned companies and their stocks.

Commercial Services and Supplies
Company Overview of Canada Revenue Agency
January 18, 2017 10:15 PM ET

Snapshot	People

Company Overview

Canada Revenue Agency (CRA) offers tax and benefits administration services to the Government of Canada. It provides tax assessment and collection, source deductions collection, voluntary disclosures assessment and processing, and Taxpayer Relief Provisions approval services. Additionally, the agency offers filing and remittance compliance, social and economic benefit, and incentive programs administration services. CRA, formerly known as Canada Customs and Revenue Agency, was founded in 1999 and is based in Ottawa, Canada.

Key Executives For Canada Revenue Agency

Mr. William V. Baker
Commissioner and Chief Executive Officer

Rebecca Rogers
Director of Communications

Mr. Richard Thorpe
Chairman of Management Board

Ms. Patricia J. Mella
Member of Management Board

Mr. Camille Belliveau
Member of Management Board

Compensation as of Fiscal Year 2016

555 MacKenzie Avenue
Ottawa, ON K1A 0L5
Canada

Phone: 613-941-3121
Fax: 613-957-7613
www.cra-arc.gc.ca

Founded in 1999

(Figure 11.1)[39]

[39]Bloomberg.com. Accessed January 16, 2017.
http://www.bloomberg.com/research/stocks/private/snapshot.asp?privcapId=6908087

CHAPTER 12

Canada Pension Ponzi

The CPP as of June, 30th 2014 has about $226B Canadian dollars' worth of holdings. A look at this portfolio helps us get a look at what types of risks are involved in the CPP and whether the Canadians 45 years and younger will ever be able to retire. The current portfolio has around 36.9%, in Currency risk mostly held in US Dollars, 41.5% held in Equities about 30% in Private by Stock Exchange 70% is invested in Public Companies traded on the Global Stock Exchanges (The biggest held stocks are in RBC Royal Bank of Canada and TD Toronto Dominion Bank. 13.9% is invested in a wide array of Real Estate and Infrastructure most of it being invested in Cash Flow investments. The rest being in Dividend and Interest accruing investment and 2.41% invested in derivatives of that. Below is a picture of the board running the CPP.[40]

Below shows you the compensation of the current leadership of the CPP.

---

[40] Actuary Reports and Special Exam Reports | CPPIB | Canada Pension Plan Investment Board. Accessed February 20, 2017. http://cppib.com/en/our-performance/exam-reports.html.

TABLE 5: SUMMARY TOTAL COMPENSATION

NAME AND POSITION	Year	Salary[1] ($) A	In-year award ($) B	Deferred awards[2] ($) C	Pension Compensation[3] value ($) D	All Other Compensation[4] ($) E	Total compensation (with Deferred Award) ($) A+B+ C+D+E	LTIP[5] payout ($) F	Total compensation (with LTIP payout) ($) A+B+ D+E+F
Mark D. Wiseman[6] President and CEO	2016	630,000	1,928,800	1,928,800	73,403	14,155	4,575,238	981,600	3,628,038
	2015	515,000	1,875,400		61,125	13,945		1,219,900	3,685,370
	2014	505,000	1,812,300		59,955	14,148		1,248,100	3,639,503
Benita Warmbold[6] SMD & CFO	2016	387,500	943,700	943,700	42,230	11,641	2,328,771	661,000	2,046,071
	2015	347,500	715,600		38,535	9,009		960,600	2,271,244
	2014	340,000	895,500		37,723	10,515		999,500	2,282,238
All amounts reported are in HKD[7]									
Mark Machin[7] SMD and Head of International, President CPPIB Asia Inc.	2016	4,800,000	14,724,900	14,724,900	432,060	1,492,609	36,174,409	6,810,800	28,260,309
	2015	3,850,000	10,047,000		346,500	1,310,578		5,334,100	20,888,178
	2014	3,500,000	7,674,200		315,812	1,184,548		8,721,500	21,396,060
Eric Wetlaufer[8] SMD & Global Head Public Market Investments	2016	460,000	1,392,700	1,392,700	51,363	29,090	3,325,852	1,680,600	3,613,752
	2015	375,000	1,451,300		42,247	19,911		1,677,900	3,566,359
	2014	367,500	1,480,100		41,436	16,274		1,087,100	2,992,410
Graeme M. Eadie[6] SMD & Global Head Real Estate Investments	2016	450,000	1,398,500	1,398,500	50,068	8,748	3,305,816	1,397,700	3,305,816
	2015	367,500	1,422,300		41,235	10,312		1,631,200	3,472,447
	2014	360,000	1,449,900		40,423	10,515		1,491,400	3,352,239
Ed Cass[6] SMD & Chief Investment Strategist	2016	430,000	1,319,100	1,319,100	47,456	6,819	3,122,475	1,360,100	3,163,475
	2015	350,000	1,362,400		38,822	6,538		1,243,400	3,001,160
	2014	336,900	1,029,100		37,310	6,747		1,253,000	2,663,052

1 One-time adjustments were made to the salaries as a result of the compensation structure redesign. Refer to the "Key changes to our compensation framework" section in the CD&A for further information.

2 The FIS deferred award represents the award value at the time of the award. The award fluctuates with the performance of the total Fund over the vesting period.

3 All other compensation includes life insurance, disability benefits, health and dental benefits, and fitness reimbursement as well as comprehensive health assessment conducted at a private medical clinic. Perquisites are limited to paid parking for officers. Mr. Machin receives a housing allowance in accordance with local market practice.

4 The LTIP was discontinued as part of the incentive plan redesign in fiscal 2015. Residual payments were paid out in fiscal 2016, and eligible employees will continue to receive payments at the end of fiscal 2017 and fiscal 2018.

5 NEO elected to defer all or part of the fiscal 2016 in-year award into the Voluntary Deferred Incentive Plan (VDIP).

6 The one year average exchange rate from HKD:CAD for the period of April 1, 2015 to March 31, 2016 is 0.169049. (Source: Bank of Canada).

7 Mr. Machin joined CPPIB on March 16, 2012. As per his employment contract, Mr. Machin received a fiscal 2013 SRFU grant of HKD 11,400,000, which vested over 3 years: 50% vested at the end of fiscal 2013 and 50% at the end of fiscal 2014. Mr. Machin also received a fiscal 2013 SLTIP (Supplemental Long Term Incentive Plan) grant of HKD 3,400,000, which vested at the end of fiscal year 2015. These amounts are reported under LTIP payout.

8 Mr. Wetlaufer joined CPPIB on June 27, 2011. As per his employment agreement, Mr. Wetlaufer's fiscal 2012 SRFU grant of $1,400,000 vested over two years, 50% paid out at the end of fiscal 2012 and 50% at the end of fiscal 2013. Mr. Wetlaufer also received an SLTIP (Supplemental Long Term Incentive Plan) grant of $350,000 in fiscal 2012, which vested at the end of fiscal year 2014.

(Figure 12.0)[41]

As you can see there is no protection against currency risk. I guess they can't really start hoarding gold as they are watched heavily by the industry. But you can see that about 84% of their entire portfolio are paper investments valued in FIAT Currency. There is a huge risk here, and if we were to hit the Currency reset button worldwide and move with a global SDR system run by the IMF we are in deep trouble as if the SDR's will need to go to a gold standard everything that is not denominated in gold backed currency will become close to worthless. Gold is an insurance against currency failure. Only about 16%

---

[41] 2016 Annual Reports Reports | CPPIB | Canada Pension Plan Investment Board. Accessed May 19, 2016.
http://www.cppib.com/documents/1355/CPPIB_F2016_Annual_Report_-_ENGLISH_May_19_2016_G0UhjTk.pdf

are in Real Estate which has some value to it, but commercial and retail sector are very dangerous to invest in also if we see currency failure. Already we see monetary velocity, which is the measure of how fast currency flows through the economy at record lows and on a downward trend. So where is the investment in solid commodities and land? These are one of the most important factors of investing in a structural fiat currency failure trend. Land located in good locations around growing cities or farmland, are holding real economic value, as they can be used to produce food for the increasing population.

Countries that hold little gold, as I have said earlier that the Bank of Canada holds no gold and that equates to 0.00% of the country's GDP compared to the EU at 2.7% and the US at 2.2%. The risk is that, when the currency system fails and the elite's moves to a gold standard worldwide. Those who sit on investments denominated in Fiat Currency will sit on worthless "Assets".

The CPP also needs constant new contributions as the baby boomers soon start to retire in full peak capacity which forces the CPP to liquidate their portfolio while needing more people contribute. Recently a move to pay more for employees in CPP contribution was announced as there is a shortfall of people able to contribute into the Pension Fund. And we 45 years and we are paying more money into the system than ever before. As the monetary system need keep this pension plan going escalates to record heights it will not make up for these increased payouts. In late 2016 Bill Morneau the current finance minister of Canada put forth new rules that increased the amount of contribution you need to pay from your salary to the CPP fund. The reason can be seen in the chart below.

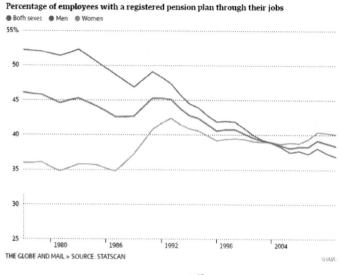

Percentage of employees with a registered pension plan through their jobs
● Both sexes ● Men ● Women

THE GLOBE AND MAIL » SOURCE: STATSCAN

(Figure 12.1)[42]

As you can see the shortfall of people having a Registered Pension Plan is the alleged reasoning for hiking the CPP contribution. I think there are more reasons for the decline in Registered Retirement Savings Plans. Number one is that, inflation is ever increasing and with stagnate wages people are getting squeezed more and their pension contributions stops. Another reason in my belief is also that people see through the scam that these government and bank run plans are. There might be more people seeing other options outside of the registered plans, giving less tax impacts and more revenue back. Many of

---

[42] "CPP reform: What's changing and how it will affect you." The Globe and Mail. Accessed January 05, 2017. https://www.theglobeandmail.com/globe-investor/retirement/cpp-reform-whats-changing-and-how-it-will-affectyou/article30551445/.

the funds that are in big funds have high fees and if you don't contribute you might lose money. The reason why people got enticed in the first place to get into the RRSP band wagon was the tax credit. What they don't think of is the heavy tax burden you will get on the back end. The government will willingly give you a tax deduction on the low front end to collect a big tax check on your larger saved up amount in your RRSP's when you retire. A lot of people have not considered the tax implications on their hard-earned money and many people I have spoken to and heard stories from several wealth managers have said they were shocked and did not calculate in the heavy tax hit. Reality settles in and many move their money away from these coercive plans.

See below for average wage increases and inflation in Canada.

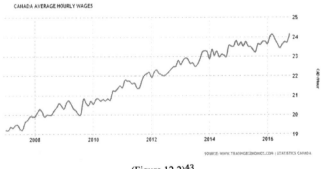

(Figure 12.2)[43]

16.94% is the official government inflation number. With salaries increasing at an average of 25% over the same time period, it all looks good, but let me add some other numbers. With household debt increasing over the same time almost 40% it shows us that instead of things

---

[43] http://www.tradingeconomics.com. Accessed July 23, 2016.

looking so bright we are seeing a deep black hole emerge in the Canadian economy.

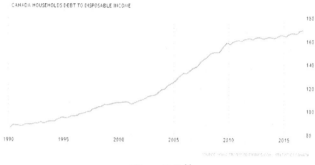

(Figure 12.3)[44]

On top of the debt, we must also calculate the taxation. So how much more do Canadians pay in taxes on an average over that time? Taxes haven't increased until 2016. They jumped quite substantially from 29% up to 33%.

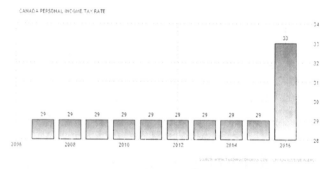

(Figure 12.4)[45]

The problem I see is that the government taxes the high business income earners and punishes them for pro-

---

[44] ibid

[45] ibid

ducing and innovating. This always drowns a society. Without a low government spending and a truly free market, there is no way out other than an eventual bankruptcy of the government as seen in Greece, Italy, Spain, Ireland and Portugal. We are getting squeezed on many fronts. The solution in my point of view is to change the monetary system and to limit government to a minimum. This will free up time, capital and creativity to put us on a brighter trajectory than today's road to ruin as many nations and governments have done before us. I suggest you read through my first book "The End of Freedom: How Our Monetary System Enslaves Us" to get a deeper insight into world history of today's monetary and economic systems.

CHAPTER 13

How the Elites Plan to Steal Your Money

What is the plan for the world and Canada included? Let's show you with a quick overview. After they did a bail out in 2008 they found out that it was very hard to take people's wealth. They had to put an apparatus in place, a control grid of legislation to seize your assets and potentially private property. We see the moves of months or yearlong martial law after terror attacks in France and Germany. The ISIS terror attacks were in Europe a perfect cover story to implement Martial Law on national levels to "protect" people from further attacks. We do know that both Germany and France have substantial economic issues caused by both over leveraged banking system and also oversized and bloated governments falling apart.

There were little wealth confiscations in 2008 other than wealth losses, but a lot of the "important" corporations and banking institutions were bailed out with a massive printing of money and swapping bad investments with new currency from central banks. All Central Banks now have an incredible sized balance sheet with investments that had gone bad bought out from mostly banks.

As bailouts have failed miserably they are looking at new ways on "saving" the world. A new tactic has emerged. Instead of letting people feel that they will be taken care of there will be an approach of Cashless Society, Martial Law, Bank Holidays, Capital Controls, Bail Ins, Wealth and Property confiscation.

Currently there are big moves around the world to create the system to make it easy to control the populace. The elites are afraid of people standing up therefore they have implemented in countries regulation that can help the government create a martial law implementation during the next economic crash. They are also working on creating cashless societies. If you want to know the elites plan in detail I suggest you need to read the book of one of the engineers behind the new game plan Kenneth Rogoff. Just to give you a background of where he comes from here is an overview of who he has worked for. He is a member of the Council of Foreign Relation since 2004; he sits on the Economic Advisory Panel of the Federal Reserve. He is a member of the National Academy of Sciences and the American Academy of Arts and Sciences and a part of the Group of Thirty often abbreviated to G30. G30 is an international body of leading financiers and academics which aims to deepen understanding of economic and financial issues and to examine consequences of decisions made in the public and private sectors related to these issues. Topical areas within the interest of the group include: the foreign exchange market, international capital markets, international financial institutions, central banks and their supervision of financial services and markets, and also macroeconomic issues such as product and labour markets.

The group is noted for its advocacy of changes in global clearing and settlement. His book *This Time Is Different: Eight Centuries of Financial Folly*, which he co-authored with Carmen Reinhart, was released in October 2009.

In *The Curse of Cash*, published in 2016, he urged that the United States phase out the 100-dollar bill, then the 50-dollar bill, then the 20-dollar bill, leaving only smaller denominations in circulation.

The book The Curse of Cash is a book you have to read. Here he suggests the plan of a cashless society, that the elite have now implemented, though in a soft way like India's current removal of the 500 and 1000 rupee bills from circulation or the calls like Rogoff and Summers of removal of high denomination bills in the US or the New Zealand suggestion of getting rid of their $100 bill. After a Cashless society, he and others have suggested to implement negative interest rates. This is you letting the bank charge you from borrowing them your money and letting them spend it on whatever they want until you take it out in Cash which you won't be able to do now with a cashless society. Cash in today's society is the last bastion of privacy and control over your own life. People deal in cash because they don't want everyone to know what they always buying a. Now in the elites view Cash is talked about to avoid taxes, it is a source of spreading disease and it is heavy to carry around and can be stolen easily by burglars. Of course, they tie it to criminal activity, which is true, but not nearly all cash is used for criminal activity. People want privacy; they don't want an electronic trail of whatever they do. Some people say I got nothing to hide. Well, good for you! I got nothing to hide as well, but I don't want to give the power to banks and governments to control my electronic bank account! What if they don't like you? Just remove the $98.883 in your account and replace it with a "0" and you are basically removed from society. This is the danger we are facing. The Cashless society is of course the start of how to control everyone. If this is successful as I have read that most societies have an implementation date of 2020.

After the cashless society, has been implemented, then the real attack on your freedoms can start. Let me tell you how this could unfold. A sudden bank holiday at one or 2 major banks in Canada come from nowhere not really, but most people would know what is coming. Capital controls like what happened in Cyprus in 2013 or Greece in 2015 where you will only have access to take out enough money out of your bank account to keep yourself with food. Of course, through the G20 FSB decisions of creating a Bail In legislation will be put in power in Cyprus which was a trailed balloon accounts under the "insured" €100k lost an average of 6.75% and 9.99% for accounts over €100k. They called it a haircut or a tax. It was a Bail In of the bank. A bail out you steals taxpayer's money and governments bail insolvent institutions out like in 2008. The bail in is your money taken from your bank account to "recapitalize" or bailing out the bank. With a cashless society you can avoid bank runs like the ones in Cyprus and Greece. Remember, it's a wonderful life? These types of bank runs happen all the time as banks have over leveraged by lending out 1:10 more money or in some cases today 1:100 more times than deposits. Suddenly people default on the un-backed debt borrowed out and the bank has lost the little money they were supposed to have in a depositor's account. When you put money in your bank account that money is not yours it is the banks. It is not yours until you want it back by spending it in a cashless society or taking out cash in the current system.

After Bail In announcement, the governments and institutions will double down. Did you think your pension was safe? If you survive on a government funded pension just say goodbye. If you have your own pension the money will most likely be frozen and you cannot touch it. There are legislations that many governments have put out in their cooperation with the G20's FSB. The major asset companies like Blackrock and others will suddenly stop you from accessing your money. This happened in smaller REIT funds and some other funds in 2008. This is to control capital flow so the crash doesn't contaminate everywhere like in 2008. After they froze your assets and bailed in your money, you are desperately trying to get your money from the bank or your pension fund private or government funded. You can't access the money. That was all you had and now you got very little to no money. Welcome to Venezuela of 2016-2017. This is not the first time of "Bail In". Governments have 100's of times before frozen money and devalued it to pay down an excessive amount of government debt. This is a little different as today there will be no central banks left that can print an excessive amount of money. Your family run to the store to hoard food because of uncertainty. If you are in the city your food supply will stop in about 3 days as that is how long grocery stores stock for. After that everyone will be for themselves. After massive money riots the food riots kick in. People that were not prepared are getting panicked. Talking to people who have survived financial collapses; food, water and precious metals were what saved people from living miserable life's barely surviving and being fully dependent on governments. But the governments if not stopped will take your private property at gunpoint if they have to in order to implement the world first global government.

As riots increase governments start implementing and launching martial law and will now roll out their militarized police force and homeland security forces that they prepared for these types of scenarios. They have been trained many times to shoot you if you don't stand in line. After Martial Law has been implemented the next step is an international monetary congress like a Bretton Woods in the 40's. The monetary system will be reformed the way the elites want and a one world currency called the Special Drawing Rights will be implemented. If you don't believe me, read the Emerging Power and Global Governance: Wither the IMF[46] from 2015. It is a white paper on how to implement the IMF's Special Drawing Rights currency on a global scale. Don't worry, you will probably never see the SDR. Their plan is to devalue all currencies to the SDR in an Argentinian way like in 2001 where a friend of mine lost 75% of the value of his money overnight. Only big corporations and nations will trade the SDR which currently derives its value from a basket of currencies. The Yen, Yuan, Euro, British Pound and US Dollar. Canada currently sits on $7.609B US Dollars' worth of SDR's held in reserves by The Bank of Canada.[47]

If enough people get educated, we can stop this as people will see that the SDR is just another form of paper Fiat

[46] Mohan , Rakesh, and Muneesh Kapur. Emerging Powers and Global Governance: Whither the IMF? Working paper no. 15/219. October 2015. Accessed April 08, 2017. http://www.imf.org/external/pubs/ft/wp/2015/wp15219.pdf.

[47] "Official International Reserves." Bank of Canada. Accessed April 08, 2017. http://www.bankofcanada.ca/rates/related/international-reserves/.

CANADA, THE GREATEST ECONOMY IN THE WORLD?• 101

Money enforced by government. As things, might worsen they have prepared camps and have hoarded weapons while the elites and governments hide in their armoured redoubts.

They will take all you have including your private property and a fascist totalitarian corporate controlled regime will emerge. Where the multinationals replace most government and we end up in a mix between Venezuela, Soviet, Hitler's Germany with a control grid that is a totalitarian regimes wet dream.

People that do not agree will be put in prison and tortured and re-educated. I have heard so many horror stories from people living in Germany WWII, Former Yugoslavia or the Soviet Union, even China and Cuba. With our current prime minister, Justin Trudeau following UN legislations like Carbon Tax implementation and praising Fidel Castro as he was a near friend of his deceased dad Pierre I think Canada has a bleak future ahead of it if we don't wake the populace up to these grim realities as history looks to repeat itself.

Don't let the government rack up debt, it will never pay off. It will only ruin the future generations coming after us. It is time to stop short-sighted politicians from destroying the future prosperity of Canada and future generations to come. It is time to limit government control, have a debt jubilee, and start from a clean sleight. With an approach of voluntary interaction with society where you are not forced into paying taxes to a government that pay themselves first instead of the people who fund them. We need to apply solutions never seen in history to make the future work and give ourselves and future generations a chance to live with prosperity and a sense of wanting to innovate and create value for society instead of keeping a system where those who take money from others win.

That been said, the elites have big plans. The implementation of a world government, one world currency and taxation is coming our way if we don't fight back. Currently there are hidden agendas through the UN Agenda 2030, Special Drawing Rights and OECD's Base Erosion and Profit shifting. The three above are world governance, one world currency and one world taxation. I will discuss about these three a little, but it would be up to you to dig deeper down the rabbit hole of control.

Starting with Agenda 2030[48], the new version of Agenda 21[49]. It started as an idea from a former Prime Minister of Norway, representing the Workers Party of Norway. The first draft was called Our Common Future: Report of the World Commission on Environment and Development. Gro Harlem Brundtland's report was the start of what is known today as Sustainable Development she got help from Manitoba, Canada's Maurice Strong. Here is a quick bio to help you understand his beliefs. Maurice Strong, as an 18-year-old Canadian from Manitoba, started work at the United Nations in 1947 as a junior officer in the UN Security Section, living with the UN Treasurer, Noah Monod. Following his exposure for bribery and corruption in the UN's Oil-for-Food scandal Maurice Strong was stripped of many of his 53 international awards and honours he had collected during his lifetime working in dual role of arch conservationist and ruthless businessman. Together, Strong and Brund-

48 http://www.un.org/pga/wp-content/uploads/sites/3/2015/08/120815_outcome-document-of-Summit-for-adoption-of-the-post-2015-development-agenda.pdf. Accessed April 10, 2017.

49https://sustainabledevelopment.un.org/content/documents/Agenda21.pdf. Accessed April 10, 2017.

tland put together the framework for UN's takeover of the local governments. You might have seen Sustainable Development being pushed in your local community. Remember that this was an idea to take over the world that came together in 1987. Today you can see it everywhere all down to the way cities and communities are planned. Many other laws have also been implemented through the UN's policy groups that are unelected and have the ultimate power to run the world. The goals that the UN laid out in 2015 are as follows:

1. No Poverty
2. Zero Hunger
3. Good Health and Well Being
4. Quality Education
5. Gender Equality
6. Clean Water and Sanitation
7. Affordable and Clean Energy
8. Decent Work and Economic Growth
9. Industry Innovation and Infrastructure
10. Reduced Inequalities
11. Sustainable Cities and Communities
12. Responsible Consumption and Production
13. Climate Action
14. Life Below Water
15. Life and Land
16. Peace, Justice and Strong Institutions
17. Partnerships for the Goals

First glance they might look like fantastic ideas. But if we take a closer look there is a big goal here. The goal is the implementation of the UN Global Government. Nation's states must die slowly as they are being merged into the UN control grid. If you don't think that there is no plan for the global government let me show you the institutions that the UN has already put in place. This global government has been growing while nation's states and citizens have unwillingly or willingly funded it through the government's contribution.

		Specialized organisations and agencies of the United Nations				
N o.	Acron yms	Agency	Headqua rters	Head	Establi shed	Com ment
1	FAO	Food and Agriculture Organization	Rome, Italy	José Graziano da Silva	1945	
2	IAEA	International Atomic Energy Agency	Vienna, Austria	Yukiya Amano	1957	Associate d agency
3	ICAO	International Civil Aviation Organization	Montrea l, Canada	Raym ond Benjamin	1947	
4	IFAD	International Fund for Agricultural Development	Rome, Italy	Kanay o.F. Nwanze	1977	
5	ILO	International Labour Organization	Geneva, Switzerland	Guy Ryder	1919	Originall y part of League of Nations
6	IMO	International Maritime Organization	London, United Kingdom	Kitack Lim	1948	

Specialized organisations and agencies of the United Nations						
N o.	Acron yms	Agency	Headqua rters	Head	Establi shed	Com ment
7	IMF	International Monetary Fund	Washing ton, D.C., United States	Christi ne Lagarde	1945	
8	ITU	International Telecommuni cation Union	Geneva, Switzerland	Hama doun Touré	1865	
9	UNESCO	United Nations Educational, Scientific and Cultural Organization	Paris, France	Irina Bokova	1945	
10	UPU	Universal Postal Union	Bern, Switzerland	Bishar Abdirahm an Hussein	1947	
11	WBG	World Bank Group	Washing ton, D.C, United States	Jim Yong Kim	1945	
12	WIPO	World Intellectual	Geneva, Switzerland	Franci s Gurry.	1974	

Specialized organisations and agencies of the United Nations						
N o.	Acron yms	Agency	Headqua rters	Head	Establi shed	Com ment
		Property Organization				
13	WMO	World Meteorologic al Organization	Geneva, Switzerland	David Grimes	1950	
14	UNWTO	United Nations World Tourism Organization	Madrid, Spain	Taleb Rifai	1974	
15	UNODC	United Nations Office on Drugs and Crime	Vienna, Austria	Yuri Fedotov	1997	
16	WHO	World Health Organization	Geneva, Switzerland	Marga ret Chan	1948	to promote mental and physical health of humanity

(Figure 13.0)

Departments and offices of the United Nations Secretariat

The United Nations Secretariat carries out the day-to-day work of the organization. It services the other principal organs of the United Nations and administers the programmes and policies laid down by them. At its head is the Secretary-General, who is appointed by the

General Assembly. The Secretariat administers several notable Offices and Departments.

No.	Acronyms	Agency	Headquarters	Head	Established	Comment
Departments and Offices of the United Nations Secretariat						
1	UNOCHA	Office for the Coordination of Humanitarian Affairs	New York City, United States	Stephen O'Brien	1991	
2	UNOOSA	United Nations Office for Outer Space Affairs	Vienna, Austria	Simonetta Di Pippo	1958	

(Figure 13.1)

Treaty organizations

The United Nations maintains, administers or has a working relationship with several organizations dedicated to the administration of a variety of international treaties and conventions. At times these perform specific administrative functions while also providing a specific forum for discussing issues around a treaty. The organizations themselves generally report to the member states of the treaty rather than to the General Assembly.

N o.	Acrony ms	Agency	Headquarters	Head	Establish ed	Comme nt
1	ISA	International al Seabed Authority	Kingston, Jamaica	Nii Allotey Odunton	1994	
2	CTBTO	Comprehen sive Nuclear-Test-Ban Treaty Organizatio n	Vienna, Austria	Lassi na Zerbo	1997 (preparato ry commissio n)	Provision al organisati on
3	OPCW	Organisatio n for the Prohibition of Chemical Weapons	The Hague, Netherlan ds	Ahm et Üzümcü	1997	Related organisati on

Table title: **Organizations with a working relationship with the United Nations**

(Figure 13.2)

Research and training institutes

There are only five officially recognised training bodies of the United Nations System. Irrespective of what does or does not constitute a United Nations organization, many other institutions serve a research or training purpose, and some are part of other organisations and funds. These are also contained below.

Research and training bodies of the United Nations						
No.	Acronyms	Agency	Headquarters	Head	Established	Comment
1	UNIDIR	United Nations Institute for Disarmament Research	Geneva, Switzerland	Theresa Hitchins	1980	
2	UNU	United Nations University	Tokyo, Japan	David M. Malone	1969	
3	UNITAR	United Nations Institute for Training and Research	Geneva, Switzerland	Sally Fagan-Wyles	1965	
4	UNRISD	United Nations Research Institute For Social Development	Geneva, Switzerland	Sarah Cook	1963	

5	UNICRI	United Nations Interregional Crime and Justice Research Institute	Turin, Italy	Jonathan Lucas	1968	
6	UNSSC	United Nations System Staff College	Turin, Italy	Jafar Javan	2002	
7	UPEACE	University for Peace	San José, Costa Rica	Francisco Rojas Aravena	1980	UN mandated
8	ICTP	International Centre for Theoretical Physics	Trieste, Italy	Fernando Quevedo	1964	IAEA, UNESCO, Italian Govt
9	IRC	Innocenti Research Centre - International Child Development Centre	Florence, Italy	Marie-Claude Martin	1988	Part of UNICEF

(Figure 13.3)

Subsidiary bodies of the General Assembly

The following entities were established by the General Assembly:

Acrony m	Agency	Headquarter s	Head	Establishe d	Commen t
ICSC	Domestic Civil Service Commissio n	New York City, United States	John P. Hamilton	1975	
ACPAQ	Advisory Committee on Post Adjustment Questions	New York City, United States	Wolfgan g Stöckl		Part of ICSC

(Figure 13.4)[50]

Wow, that is a lot to digest isn't it. Well your tax money has helped this grow whether you like it or not. The UN has all the tools they need to create a global government, but it needs to work slowly. Saying that we will have a global government can cause people to rise and fight back. As we have seen with Brexit and the rise of Populists like Trump, Le Pen, Wilders and many others are fighting back without thinking of why they got them to believe in the first place. People love their freedom even in communist societies if the state becomes too heavy they will rise up. It is a natural force of freedom of the individual that is the underlying principle. Of course, not all the populist has great ideas in my point of view, but they want that freedom from a top-heavy government that have stopped to work for the people and only works for the elites, their corporations and political self-interest.

Now that been said, how do you implement such a bold plan? Again incremental, but every now and then a

---

[50]http://www.un.org/en/aboutun/structure/pdfs/UN_System_Chart_30June2015. pdf. Accessed April 15, 2017.

crisis is arising and as Rahm Emanuel, former Obama Advisor and now Mayor of Chicago said "Don't let a good crisis go to waste." There is a lot of evidence of a collapsing monetary system. In the 20th century dictators like Hitler used the collapse of the German Reichsmarks to get into power. In a crisis where you lose your house, your savings and what you had worked so hard to gain. People become desperate and they will vote for anyone who promises them everything or something for free. What you must understand is that the government is supposed to be there for you not the other way around. When the government becomes the employer, the parent and the controller over your freedoms you have lost. You have now entered the end game of any collectivist system Dictatorship and Communism.

After these crises in our monetary systems, there is a vacuum created. People lost what they had and are angry at their controllers, the bankers, together with the government, they always end up running any unaccounted monetary system to the ground.

Now there is need for a new system, a Global Bretton Woods agreement. The UN has a solution for that. The International Monetary Fund (IMF)[51]. The name is deceiving. They are a global Central Bank and they have a currency the Special Drawing Right. For deeper research on this topic, read their working papers. Emerging Powers and Global Governance: Whither the IMF? Here they go through how to make the SDR the new global currency only available for Elites, Multilateral Corporations and Nation Governments. We the populace will be left with devalued local currencies that will then be

---

[51] Mohan , Rakesh, and Muneesh Kapur. Emerging Powers and Global Governance: Whither the IMF? Working paper no. 15/219. October 2015. Accessed April 08, 2017. http://www.imf.org/external/pubs/ft/wp/2015/wp15219.pdf.

pegged to the value of the SDR. They have no plan to share this currency with us. As a matter of fact, the IMF has already printed as of January, 31st 2017, 204,157,943,411[52] of the currency. In my point of view the IMF is nothing else but a loan shark organization. They borrow money to heavily indebted countries or to corrupt world leaders and then as the elites took the nation's money as the country defaults on the IMF loan and the sharks circle the country with its friends and loot all the resources and infrastructure for next to nothing. I do not know if the elites will back their currency with gold or if they will just create another fiat currency that will fail again. They can of course after the collapse as described above implement their e-currencies based on the Blockchain currency system of Bitcoin but under central control. Finally, they have their electronic control over all your money. They can remove you if they don't like you. Just like the movie In Time with Justin Timberlake. When a currency becomes fully electronic all your wealth is now owned by the banks. I have talked earlier in the book that when you deposit your money into a bank account you don't own that money anymore. It is lent to the bank and they can do whatever they like with your money.

As the currency control grid falls in place the next step is then forced taxation. This is already falling into place with the help of the G20 working group. They put in their working paper called *supporting the Development of more Effective Tax Systems.*
"A REPORT TO THE G-20 DEVELOPMENT WORKING GROUP BY THE IMF, OECD, UN AND WORLD

---

[52] "SDR Allocations and Holdings for all members as of January 31, 2017." International Monetary Fund. Accessed April 23, 2017.
https://www.imf.org/external/np/fin/tad/extsdr1.aspx.

BANK"[53]. This report came out and then the governments favourite way to act came into play with the Hegelian Dialectic of Problem (Tax Evasion aka. The Panama Papers), Reaction (The G20 Working group) and the Solution Action Plan on Base Erosion and Profit Shifting[54] or BEPS as they like to call it. I predicted that this would happen as I saw the Panama Papers as a push for global taxation. Doing a little research, I found the G20 working group paper and made the connection. The elites usually don't hide their plans they are accessible, but you need to know what to look for. In both the working paper and the BEPS policy they talk about how to come after multilateral corporations that hide money from national governments. But if you take a closer look into this program, it can easily be turned into a global taxation system under the UN. I will stop there as I have already water boarded you with too much information. I do think that it is very important that you do your own research. I have given you the insight into the plan. If you want to become an expert do your own research and make your own conclusions. But I will tell you, anger might arise as you understand more on what they think about you as an individual and their plans for an even bigger government. I highly suggest you join organizations like the one I am a part of[55]. This way you can help change Canada and the world to a better place.

---

[53]A report to the g-20 development working group by the IMF, OECD, UN and World Bank, *Supporting the Development of*
More Effective Tax Systems,https://www.imf.org/external/np/g20/pdf/110311.pdf Accessed April 23, 2017.

[54] OECD (2013), Action Plan on Base Erosion and Profit Shifting, OECD Publishing. https://www.oecd.org/ctp/BEPSActionPlan.pdf

[55] http://www.freedomforceinternational.org, http://www.theeconomictruth.org or http://www.worldalternativemedia.com

CHAPTER 14

Solutions and Final Thoughts

I want to share with you through my analysis of the 13 points I made in this book. Since I started this book there has been multiple developments. As I write, the election of our current Prime Minister Justin Trudeau from the Liberal Party of Canada and his squandering of money using the Canadian taxpayers as a slush fund to create an even bigger government than his predecessor Stephen Harper. The debt is out of control with an approximate $32B+ deficit spending. There is no way the Canadian government debt will ever get paid off! It is impossible as we would have to raise taxes to UK's 60's level or US 30's levels, when they had a top tax bracket of 90-95%. That's a total loss of their freedom. Below is a short analysis of the prior chapters and how you can fight against and protect yourself for the upcoming turmoil.

1. Bank Leverage

Get out of the banking system options here are: Bitcoin (Crypto Currencies), Gold, Land, Private Equity, Business, Fine art, Food, Water and Cash. Real Estate if you know what type of Real Estate is good at the time. Start to create a true diversity in your investments not the one that your financial advisor tells you about. Banks that have high leverage end up with collapsing debt under them and as it happened in Cyprus they might implement a bank holiday and suddenly you have less money in your bank account when the bank reopens from Bail Ins or loss of deposits you thought were insured.

2. Bail In

Bail in risk can be mitigated by mostly doing the above, but also moving into a smaller local bank. Now do remember that Credit Unions also have insurance that is insufficient if a major bank liquidity squeeze happens.

3. Deposit Insurance

Don't think you will be saved as only 0.39% of all deposits under $100k is protected from a banking system crash and the Bail In enforcement. Watch out for your money in government controlled pension plans like RRSP's and other plans. They give you the incentive of tax deduction upfront, but you will pay big on a very large sum at the back end as it is taxed as income on money you already paid taxes from through income tax. They can also freeze your assets through the G20's FSB (Financial Stability Board)'s Bail-in legislation created in Brisbane 2014.

4. Central Bank Reserves

Don't believe that your government and banks will fix things. The Canadian government and banking system will have to deal with the worst possible hand, as Canadian Gold reserves are 0%, which will pale when compared with the US, Russia and the EU all over 2.2%. If a gold standard is yet again to be enforced those who sit on the least gold lose their power in the global economy and Canada might not be a G7 member ever again. May be a G80? Don't ever trust banks and governments to take care of you as they have shown over 42 times throughout the 20th century that they failed to do! The Central Banking scheme comes and goes throughout time as the populace forgets history and the bankers repeat history by starting up a systematic fraud as soon as we have forgotten their past shenanigans.

5. The Way Government in Canada Borrow Money.

If you had the chance to borrow money at 0.5% or 2.5% when you borrow billions of dollars what would be your choice? Obvious, isn't it??? To further elaborate on this, I am a Voluntaryist and I believe no Government should borrow money or even exist.

6. Banking and investment fees

Below is an illustration for you, if you are putting the sum of $380k, over a period of 25 years you have given the bankers a fee of $566k although you have $1.28M you could have had almost $2M and that is the amount that's been stolen from you. And then you had your money in a Canadian RRSP (Registered Retirement Savings Plan) so you will be hit with massive taxes between

20-40%. Then you are looking at $1M at the low end that you sit with using the bankers and government retirement system. On the other hand, several rich individuals are using insurance instruments the same way banks run their daily business sitting with more money and completely tax free. See the Picture below for illustration of a basic mutual fund:

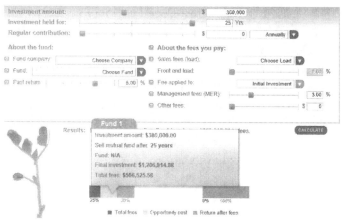

(Figure 14.0)[56]

You need to find alternatives. Become financially literate, so you can manage your own money. Having someone else taking care of your hard-earned money can be very risky. It is time for you to take charge and ask all the hard questions many of the ones I have raised in this book so you can find the right person for the job if you don't want to manage the money yourself or if you simply can't. Learn about other investment methods like Infinite Banking and Wealth insurance like gold and silver.

[56]http://www.getsmarteraboutmoney.ca/en/tools_and_calculators/calculators/Pages/mutual-fund-fee-calculator.aspx#.WIBIUPkrLIU Accessed November 10, 2016.

7. Money Supply

This one is obvious. Money supply is always increasing to pay off the interest accumulated which needs new money to get paid off. This is a vicious cycle that always ends in misery as there will never be enough money to pay off the interest on the debt created. Even if we pay off all the debt in existence that means all money there will still be a ton of interest owed on that money that can never be paid back and the Ponzi scheme is revealed!!! I post every quarter update on the money supply of about 70 countries and it doesn't surprise me at all that in 95%-99% of the cases, countries money supply has increased! We need to understand the historical implications of a fiat debt based system with fractional reserve lending. It always fails. The time frame of currency collapse is just a little different to the average currency when paper fiat usually lasts less than 40 years. We are on borrowed times. To get the full scope of what I am talking about read first book on monetary history.

8. Real Estate Construction as a Part of GDP

Real Estate price is always a sign of debt increase. Today we are seeing a boost in Real Estate prices. What is really boosting the prices? It is an underlying debt bubble and foreign investors pouring their money into some of the few places left with a real estate market going up and up and up. Norway and the UK have similar markets. The UK is more in trouble as they have government loan welfare paying 20% of your house mortgage value. This keeps the fake price of real estate in an upward trend until it is not enough with 20% of your mortgage paid by the government and 30-40% and more and more. In Canada Construction and Lending + surrounding businesses almost equates to 25% of the country's GDP and this is excessive. In a market downturn, the new houses are overvalued and they have a mark-up on them to make the builders money.

Phoenix, Florida, Detroit and other real estate market before they busted was over built and the banks were pushing for people who could barely afford new houses. And the upper middleclass foreigners are also buying houses to get their money out of the country. This only fuels the bubble further and I am seeing locally more building and many foreigners buying houses, but don't live there.

---

9. Debt

Money = Debt. This is the formula that you are not been taught in school. Over 98% of money in circulation today is debt, and on that debt, there is interest due. How do pay off that interest? You need to create more debt or else face depression with bankruptcies and foreclosures! That is just how the system works! Debt is increasing simultaneously with the Money supply! Debt is not the killer but it is the interest that keeps us in the need for a continuous growth pattern. That is why you hear politicians talk about economic growth all the time as that is the only antidote to keep the Ponzi scheme from falling apart. Yes, growth is possible, but infinite growth can only work if we have a supply of infinite resources, which this beautiful world does not have. It is finite and we need to make sure we use our resources wisely as they are the ones keeping us alive!! Stay out of debt.

10. Commodities and Real Money

Canada has commodities, but lack real money. We have oil, potash, gold, food and uranium. We have farmland amass, but we do need to understand that these real resources are the backbone of an economy as we need energy and food to keep us alive. Any boom in energy available creates a boom in a civilization, human or animal. A boom in oxygen during the earth's history created a massive boom in population of animals and/or insects during the past. Here is a little history lesson for you.

The concentration of atmospheric oxygen is often cited as a possible contributor to large-scale evolutionary phenomena, such as the origin of the multicellular Ediacara biota, the Cambrian explosion, trends in animal body size, and other extinction and diversification events.

The large size of insects and amphibians in the Carboniferous period, where oxygen reached 35% of the atmosphere, has been attributed to the limiting role of diffusion in these organisms' metabolism. But Haldane's essay points out that it would only apply to insects. However, the biological basis for this correlation is not firm, and many lines of evidence show that oxygen concentration is not size-limiting in modern insects. Interestingly, there is no significant correlation between atmospheric oxygen and maximum body size elsewhere in the geological record. Ecological constraints can better explain the diminutive size of post-Carboniferous dragonflies - for instance, the appearance of flying competitors such as pterosaurs and birds and bats.

Today the boom in population we have is also based on energy. Carbon energies from coal, oil and gas. We will see depletion in these resources and that will be a hint of the end of our living standards as we know it. Many of the things we use today especially plastic is a bi product of oil[57].

Looking at our economic system and commodities we will see that Commodities are finite and cannot be recreated after they are gone. Debt can and you can print Quadrillions of it, but you won't increase the supply of a commodity or food unless you find more soil to grow on or manage to harvest Helium from another planet.

Back to Canada, the Central and Western provinces have a lot of access to commodities and food through the access to agricultural land. Manitoba, Saskatchewan, Alberta and some parts of Northern Ontario and BC have resources and farmland. These provinces are more resistant to downturns as the financial sector can fail there, but there will still be energy and food available to their residents. During a crisis, these provinces might be safer than ex. Quebec and Most parts of Ontario.

The question now is, will the commodity province's secession from Canada during the next collapse as they feed the Canadian government through agricultural, energy taxes and royalties.

11. The CRA (Canada Revenue Agency) The Tax collectors

Taxes usually come into play to help a country go to war and this is no different in Canada and others. Taxes are one of the ways government make income to go to war and they can also print money. The truth is that today, Governments print money through deficit spending and then need to tax us more to pay off their unsustaina-

---

[57] "Carboniferous." Wikipedia. Accessed November 30, 2016. https://en.wikipedia.org/wiki/Carboniferous.

ble debt, which they cannot pay down, but only pay interest on. CRA is a Private corporation with Government benefits that is set as the government enforces of tax collection. A Crown Corporation is very like a SOE in China. State Owned Enterprises have the governments backing them and giving them access to cheap money and deals.

The truth is that CRA is taking advantage of its position, trying to scare people into paying more taxes to give themselves better revenues. If we do need to pay taxes. We can cut the government to a minimum and pay very little taxes. Many countries around the world with fewer resources have way less taxes and that means we can too. Government will continue to grow until it has consumed the last taxable dollar in the private sector and then it will collapse back on itself.

12. CPP (Canada Pension Plan)

We look at the assets held in the Canadian pension plan and it became apparent that they have a lot of Fiat Currency denominated assets mostly derived from the real thing. The CPP is not the same as the Oil Fund of Norway or several other Sovereign Wealth Funds where they get money from the half state owned Oil or Natural Resource companies the CPP gets their increased supply of money from their own people which pay a set amount from their paychecks every one of them to contribute into the common pot. The issue here is that they are taking money directly from the people instead of taking a limited supply of profit from their Crown Corporations profits instead.

On top of that during a Fiat Currency failure many of their holdings that are denominated in FIAT and that are paper investments will become worthless or close to it.

As Fiat only holds its value until we stop believing in it. It is all a game of confidence. When a Fiat currency gets a loss of confidence from the people it was forced upon it will rapidly lose value as it will most likely need to be printed into oblivion and only things of real value will be valuable. These items would be real businesses not paper shares in them, Gold and Silver, other commodities not shares in their companies and at last land. By land I mean usable land not land based on consumption which is a big part of their holdings through their investments in Retail Shopping Centers. You are better off making your own plan and not letting governments steal your money.

Canada is not the Switzerland that we hear in the news and it is only held up by a house of debt cards that can collapse at any given time.

Maybe reconsider what you think is a great investment and see how you can mitigate your wealth's loss when the structural cracks make the whole societal and monetary structure come down.

I hope I informed you enough to start looking into what information you build your paradigm on.

After we have taken a deeper look at the so-called booming economy of Canada, we can clearly see a lot of signs that should worry us and politicians should talk about. We rarely hear anything other than how corrupt politicians in Canada are as they over use money and outright steal sometimes. How about asking the leadership in Canada about these 12 points? How about you get your friends together and start political parties or organizations to make a change possible? Or how about starting to look at ways to protect yourself from what smells and looks like a coming failure of our current monetary system. It is not a surprise that we see these problems as many of our current issues with Debt, Bank Leverage, Money Supply and ever increasing Taxes are not a new issue. Debt issues go far back and in history we learn about how Usury was banned in histories from the old parts of the bible. Usury is the charge of interest as you borrow money and even Jesus was onto the bankers with their early Ponzi schemes when he chased the money changers out of the temple. I don't necessarily see all interest as bad. If you had a 100% backing of the money you borrowed to someone and they would create something of value or innovate something while paying you back in simple interest.

The Mississippi Bubble was caused by over printing of shares diluting their value. The Assignat during the French revolution were destroyed by the same principles as today's banking system is struggling with.

What will happen through any Ponzi scheme is the hockey stick moment through exponential growth. This Exponential growth science is very important as it explains how any Fiat currency ends in a death defying moment if we always want growth as the Central Bankers want today.

Bankers earn money in compounding interest, but they give you simple interest. The difference is that compounding interest is always accumulating and simple interest is a percentage of a sum one time and it is not accumulating. This makes the world unfair for those who borrow in compounding interest and save in simple interest. The banks do the total opposite! That is why they always win in the bank run Fractional Reserve Lending system! Well in Canada the fractional lending does not exist because Canadian banks have a zero-reserve policy.

I have laid out some of the most valuable points you could learn about the Canadian economy. Now it is your responsibility to act and make sure that you share these solutions and ideas with other people.

The future of our civilization is in limbo and without a move away from the current failing system we will not be able to change. Let me finish with a quote from Winston Churchill

"The farther back you can look, the farther forward you are likely to see."

John Thore Stub Sneisen
CEO
The Economic Truth

References

Page11-12: Source Working Paper 97-8 / Document de travail 97-8: Implementation of Monetary Policy in a Regime with Zero Reserve Requirements: by Kevin Clinton
Page12: Source: SNL Financial; Compustat; Bloomberg; national financial regulators; McKinsey Global Institute
Page13: Bloomberg Research
Page14:https://www.policyalternatives.ca/sites/default/files/uploads/publications/National%20Office/2012/04/Big%20Banks%20Big%20Secret.pdf
Page16:https://www.policyalternatives.ca/sites/default/files/uploads/publications/National%20Office/2012/04/Big%20Banks%20Big%20Secret.pdf
Page17:https://www.policyalternatives.ca/sites/default/files/uploads/publications/National%20Office/2012/04/Big%20Banks%20Big%20Secret.pdf
Page19: Source Canada Action Plan Budget 2013: http://www.budget.gc.ca/2013/doc/plan/budget2013-eng.pdf
Page21: Source Canada Action Plan Budget 2016: http://www.budget.gc.ca/2016/docs/plan/budget2016-en.pdf
Page24: Source CDIC webpage: http://www.cdic.ca/en/about-cdic/Pages/default.aspx
Source CDIC webpage: http://www.cdic.ca/en/about-cdic/Pages/default.aspx
Page28: Prudent Preparation: The Evolution of Unconventional Monetary Policies Remarks Stephen S. Poloz – Governor at The Empire Club of Canada. Toronto, Canada. 8 December 2015
Page30:http://www.bankofcanada.ca/rates/related/international-reserves/
Page36:http://www.bankofcanada.ca/wp-content/uploads/2010/11/seigniorage.pdf
Page41: Power Corporation of Canada Organizational chart. https://www.powercorporation.com/en/companies/organization-chart/

Page53:http://www.zerohedge.com/sites/default/files/images/user5/imageroot/images/Silver%20content.jpg
Page54: Numbers from Royal Canadian Mint
Page55:http://www.tradingeconomics.com
Page57:http://www.tradingeconomics.com
Page58:http://www.tradingeconomics.com
Page63: Source Department of Finance, Canada: 2016 Update of Long-Term Economic and Fiscal Projections
Page65: Source, Levi Economics Institute
Page66: http://www.investorsfriend.com/canadian-gdp-canadian-imports-and-exports/
Page68:http://www.bankofcanada.ca/wp-content/uploads/2016/06/fsr-june2016.pdf
Page70:https://www.bloomberg.com/news/articles/2017-04-17/bank-of-montreal-to-offer-mbs-as-canada-shrinks-mortgage-support?cmpId=flipboard
https://en.wikipedia.org/wiki/Subprime_mortgage_crisis
Page71:https://markets.newyorkfed.org/soma/download/739/mbs?client=GUI
Page72: Google Stocks
Page 73:http://www.zerohedge.com/news/2017-04-26/canadas-housing-bubble-explodes-its-biggest-mortgage-lender-crashes-most-history
Page74:https://www.cmhc-schl.gc.ca/en/corp/nero/nere/2017/2017-04-26-1200.cfm?utm_source=twitter-main&utm_medium=link&utm_campaign=mac#mediaDownload
Page77:http://www.tradingeconomics.com
Stats Canada
Page78:http://www.tradingeconomics.com
Page 79:http://www.tradingeconomics.com
Page 83: Source: Wikipedia
Page 84: Huffington Post
Page 86: Source WORLD GOLD COUNCIL

Page92: http://cas-ncr-nter03.cas-satj.gc.ca/portal/page/portal/tcc-cci_Eng/About/Full_history
Page97: http://www.bloomberg.com/research/stocks/private/snapshot.asp?privcapId=6908087
Page98: http://cppib.com/en/our-performance/exam-reports.html
Page99: http://www.cppib.com/documents/1355/CPPIB_F2016_Annual_Report_-_ENGLISH_May_19_2016_G0UhjTk.pdf
Page101: Globe and Mail and STATSCAN
Page103: http://www.tradingeconomics.com
http://www.tradingeconomics.com
Page104: http://www.tradingeconomics.com
Page112: http://www.imf.org/external/pubs/ft/wp/2015/wp15219.pdf
http://www.bankofcanada.ca/rates/related/international-reserves/
Page114: http://www.un.org/pga/wp-content/uploads/sites/3/2015/08/120815_outcome-document-of-Summit-for-adoption-of-the-post-2015-development-agenda.pdf
https://sustainabledevelopment.un.org/content/documents/Agenda21.pdf
Page124: http://www.un.org/en/aboutun/structure/pdfs/UN_System_Chart_30June2015.pdf
Page126: Emerging Powers and Global Governance: Whither the IMF?
https://www.imf.org/external/np/fin/tad/extsdr1.aspx
Page137: https://www.imf.org/external/np/g20/pdf/110311.pdf
https://www.oecd.org/ctp/BEPSActionPlan.pdf
Page128: http://www.freedomforceinternational.org
http://www.theeconomictruth.org
http://www.worldalternativemedia.com
Page132: http://www.getsmarteraboutmoney.ca/en/tools_and_calculators/calculators/Pages/mutual-fund-fee-calculator.aspx#.WIBIUPkrLIU
Page 136: Wikipedia

Suggested Reading

The History of Fiat Paper Money - Ralph T. Foster
Rich Dad, Poor Dad - Robert T. Kiyosaki
Planet Ponzi - Mitch Feierstein
Investing in Gold and Silver - Michael Maloney
The Creature from Jekyll Isle - G. Edward Griffin
Currency Wars and the Death of Money - James G. Rickards
Strategic Vision - Zbigniew Brzezinski
Governing the World - Mark Mazower
Think and Grow Rich - Napoleon Hill
The End of the Free Market - Ian Bremmer
The Devil's Derivatives - Nicholas Dunbar
The Economics Book - DK Publishing
The Law of Connection - Michael J. Losier
The Law of Attraction - Michael J. Losier
Coined - Kabir Sehgal
Think Big - Donald Trump and Bill Zanker
Leadership Gold - John C. Maxwell
Outliers - Malcom Gladwell
The Republic of Plato - Allan Bloom
Rich Woman - Kim Kiyosaki
Guide to Investing - Robert T. Kiyosaki
Why We Want You to Be Rich - Donald Trump and Robert T. Kiyosaki
Rich Dad's Conspiracy of The Rich - Robert T. Kiyosaki
Retire Young Retire Rich - Robert T. Kiyosaki
Rich Woman - Kim Kiyosaki
The Secret - Rhonda Byrne

7 Principles of Highly Effective People - Stephen R. Covey
The Holy Bible
Jesus - Deepak Chopra
Excuses Be Gone - Wayne W. Dyer
The Four Agreements - Don Miguel Ruiz
The Mastery of Love - Don Miguel Ruiz
Awaken the Giant Within - Anthony Robbins
Increase Your Financial IQ - Robert T. Kiyosaki
Death of Money - James G. Rickards
The New Case for Gold - James G. Rickards
The Road to Ruin - James G. Rickards
The End of Freedom: How Our Monetary System Enslaves Us - John Thore Stub Sneisen
The Exchange Stabilization Fund: Slush Money or War Chest - C. Randall Henning
The Curse of Cash - Kenneth Rogoff
FED UP - Danielle DiMartino Booth
The Sale of a Lifetime - Harry S. Dent Jnr
Risk Your Global Guide - Janet M. Tavakoli
The Age of Sustainable Development - Jeffrey Sachs
The Making of The President 2016 - Roger Stone
Users Guide to the SDR
IMF Treasury Department

Disclaimer and/or Legal Notice

About The Author

John Sneisen grew up in Norway and says he had been brainwashed by the collectivist agenda until he read Rich Dad, Poor Dad, by Robert Kiyosaki. John is now a passionate advocate of individualism. He is the founder of an organization called The Economic Truth, with over 10,000 followers in more than thirty countries. It analyzes economic events and hosts workshops on monetary history. John is the author of The End of Freedom: How Our Monetary System Enslaves Us. He is a co-founder of a The Manitoba Party in Manitoba, Canada and an Economic Analyst with World Alternative Media one of Canadas biggest Alternative

Media News channels. John has a goal to awaken millions of people around the world to the truths of money, commodities, and civilizations. He is a member of the Freedom Force Leadership Council. He has also been inducted into the Freedom Force International Hall of Fame together with notable people like Robert T. Kiyosaki, Mike Adams, Lord Christopher Moncton, Catherine Austin Fitts, Ty Bollinger, G. Edward Griffin and many others.

CPSIA information can be obtained
at www.ICGtesting.com
Printed in the USA
LVOW10s1035061217
558605LV00022BA/1128/P